Nature and Ethics Across Geographical, Rhetorical and Human Borders

How we dispose of our rubbish, choose the foods we buy, enjoy art, relate to our families and think about ourselves are just a few of the ways that ideas about nature shape our everyday ethical decisions. Nature and 'natural facts' have long been used to make sense of why we act a certain way. Nature is a concept with great power: when we describe something as 'natural' or 'unnatural', it has a moral force and political consequences. We see this in moral panics about genetically modified foods, the spread of government-enforced waste recycling schemes, concerns about assisted reproductive technologies. Our ideas about what is natural shape our ethical thinking, in terms of how people live (or want to live) their lives, but also in guiding our sense of morality, justice and truth.

The idea of naturalness is essential to grasping Anglo-American cultures. Throughout history and in different places, nature has had different forms, meanings and moral valences. It is a knowable fact, but at the same time almost a divine principle that is ultimately unfathomable. Yet with the rise of new technologies, there is increasing uncertainty about what we claim to be natural, who we are, how we are related to each other and how we should live.

This book examines how ideas about nature and ethics overlap and separate across cultural, species, geographic and moral boundaries. It compares the varied ways in which nature and ideas of naturalness pervade all aspects of people's lives, from family relationships, to the production and consumption of food, to ideas about scientific truth. In a world of increasing uncertainty, nature remains a powerful concept: the ultimate reference point, invested with profound moral authority to guide our ethical behaviour.

This book was originally published as a special issue of *Ethnos: Journal of Anthropology*.

Katharine Dow is a Senior Research Associate in the Reproductive Sociology Research Group at the University of Cambridge, UK. Her main research interest is the ethical dilemmas and questions provoked by reproduction and assisted reproductive technologies.

Victoria Boydell is an Affiliated Scholar in the Reproductive Sociology Research Group at the University of Cambridge, UK. Her main research interest is social and cultural dynamics around contraceptive technologies.

Nature and Ethics Across Geographical, Rhetorical and Human Borders

Edited by
Katharine Dow and Victoria Boydell

LONDON AND NEW YORK

First published 2018
by Routledge
2 Park Square, Milton Park, Abingdon, Oxon, OX14 4RN, UK

and by Routledge
711 Third Avenue, New York, NY 10017, USA

Routledge is an imprint of the Taylor & Francis Group, an informa business

© 2018 Taylor & Francis

All rights reserved. No part of this book may be reprinted or reproduced or utilised in any form or by any electronic, mechanical, or other means, now known or hereafter invented, including photocopying and recording, or in any information storage or retrieval system, without permission in writing from the publishers.

Trademark notice: Product or corporate names may be trademarks or registered trademarks, and are used only for identification and explanation without intent to infringe.

British Library Cataloguing in Publication Data
A catalogue record for this book is available from the British Library

ISBN 13: 978-1-138-57190-7

Typeset in Adobe Caslon Pro
by RefineCatch Limited, Bungay, Suffolk

Publisher's Note
The publisher accepts responsibility for any inconsistencies that may have arisen during the conversion of this book from journal articles to book chapters, namely the possible inclusion of journal terminology.

Disclaimer
Every effort has been made to contact copyright holders for their permission to reprint material in this book. The publishers would be grateful to hear from any copyright holder who is not here acknowledged and will undertake to rectify any errors or omissions in future editions of this book.

Contents

Citation Information — vii
Notes on Contributors — ix

Introduction: Nature and Ethics Across Geographical, Rhetorical and Human Borders — 1
Katharine Dow & Victoria Boydell

1. 'Natural' Breastfeeding in Comparative Perspective: Feminism, Morality, and Adaptive Accountability — 19
Charlotte Faircloth

2. The Ethics of Patenting and Genetically Engineering the Relative Hāloa — 44
Mascha Gugganig

3. Snared: Ethics and Nature in Animal Protection — 68
Adam Reed

4. 'A Nine-Month Head-Start': The Maternal Bond and Surrogacy — 86
Katharine Dow

5. A Response to the Issues Raised in the Special Edition of *Ethnos* — 105
Alana Jelinek

Index — 113

Citation Information

The chapters in this book were originally published in *Ethnos: Journal of Anthropology*, volume 82, issue 1 (February 2017). When citing this material, please use the original page numbering for each article, as follows:

Introduction
Nature and Ethics Across Geographical, Rhetorical and Human Borders
Katharine Dow & Victoria Boydell
Ethnos: Journal of Anthropology, volume 82, issue 1 (February 2017), pp. 1–18

Chapter 1
'Natural' Breastfeeding in Comparative Perspective: Feminism, Morality, and Adaptive Accountability
Charlotte Faircloth
Ethnos: Journal of Anthropology, volume 82, issue 1 (February 2017), pp. 19–43

Chapter 2
The Ethics of Patenting and Genetically Engineering the Relative Hāloa
Mascha Gugganig
Ethnos: Journal of Anthropology, volume 82, issue 1 (February 2017), pp. 44–67

Chapter 3
Snared: Ethics and Nature in Animal Protection
Adam Reed
Ethnos: Journal of Anthropology, volume 82, issue 1 (February 2017), pp. 68–85

CITATION INFORMATION

Chapter 4
'A Nine-Month Head-Start': The Maternal Bond and Surrogacy
Katharine Dow
Ethnos: Journal of Anthropology, volume 82, issue 1 (February 2017), pp. 86–104

Chapter 5
A Response to the Issues Raised in the Special Edition of Ethnos
Alana Jelinek
Ethnos: Journal of Anthropology, volume 82, issue 1 (February 2017), pp. 105–112

For any permission-related enquiries please visit:
http://www.tandfonline.com/page/help/permissions

Notes on Contributors

Victoria Boydell is an Affiliated Scholar in the Reproductive Sociology Research Group at the University of Cambridge, UK. Her main research interest is social and cultural dynamics around contraceptive technologies.

Katharine Dow is a Senior Research Associate in the Reproductive Sociology Research Group at the University of Cambridge, UK. Her main research interest is the ethical dilemmas and questions provoked by reproduction and assisted reproductive technologies.

Charlotte Faircloth is a Lecturer at the UCL Institute of Education, London, UK.

Mascha Gugganig is a Postdoctoral Researcher at the Munich Center for Technology in Society, Technical University of Munich, Germany.

Alana Jelinek is a Research Fellow in the School of Creative Arts, University of Hertfordshire, UK.

Adam Reed is a Senior Lecturer at the Department of Social Anthropology, University of St Andrews, UK.

Introduction: Nature and Ethics Across Geographical, Rhetorical and Human Borders

Katharine Dow & Victoria Boydell

The nature–culture dichotomy is perhaps one of the most critical legacies of anthropological thought. Nature has long occupied a position of vital importance in the way in which people are understood to imagine their own and others' worlds. Given this, it is not surprising that nature has been employed by anthropologists as an analytical heuristic and, historically, as an ultimate reference point from which to make sense of human behaviour. Nature is, also, a concept with great power and rhetorical weight for the people who anthropologists encounter in the field, not least in the Western world. Diverse examples from moral panics about genetically modified foods, to the spread of government-enforced waste recycling schemes, to concerns about 'reproductive tourism' show that claims about nature are never politically, emotionally or morally neutral. For many, notions of naturalness structure ethical choices, both in terms of how people live (or want to live) their lives and in guiding our sense of right and wrong, justice and truth.

In 2012, artist and designer Ai Hasegawa exhibited her award-winning piece, 'I wanna deliver a shark...' at the Royal College of Art's *Design for the Real World* exhibition in London. The main exhibit was an anatomical model of a human uterus with a shark foetus inside it (Figure 1). Hasegawa explains in her own words:

> This project approaches the problem of human reproduction in an age of over-population and environmental crisis. With potential food shortages and a population of nearly nine[1] billion people, would a new mother consider incubating and giving birth to an endangered species such as a shark, tuna or dolphin? This project introduces a new argument for giving birth to our food to satisfy our demands for nutrition

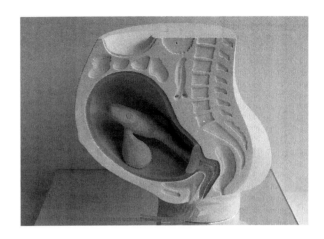

Figure 1. *'I wanna deliver a shark . . . '*, Hasegawa, 2012. Photo by artist, with permission.

and childbirth and discusses some of the technical details of how that might be possible. (Ai Hasegawa's website, accessed 19 February 2014)

Hasegawa's speculative design work proffers a radical rethinking of the human exploitation of natural resources, it razes the boundaries between species and presents a fundamental challenge to our ideas about motherhood. The idea of a woman giving birth to a shark, which she might later eat, or which might even eat her, pushes forcefully at the borders of the natural and the ethical. Like the papers in this special issue, Hasegawa's work points to questions with enormous significance: what counts as (un)natural? What happens when we cross species boundaries? What are the consequences of playing with life and death? What are humans' responsibilities to the natural world? Her work also reminds us that every scientific and medical innovation has a history and that often even the most challenging technologies have become normalised.

As Hasegawa's work viscerally reminds us, describing something as unnatural marks it as uncanny, dubious and even taboo. This is not to say that naturalness is treated as unproblematically ethical: it still has its teeth and claws, yet there is a strong implication in contemporary representations of nature within the Western world that it is, at least, fundamentally authentic. In Western epistemologies, nature is relationally defined, often paired dichotomously with culture, and the relationship between them shifts, as culture controls nature, yet nature is prior to and underlies culture. The relationship is not static but, rather, a continuous process of transformation, a changing hierarchy in which meanings shift depending on the formulation of control.

In *After Nature*, an analysis of kinship and nature in the late twentieth-century England, Strathern (1992) shows the continuous tension between nature and culture in modern thought, as society is framed as descending from nature but at the same time is different from nature because it is socialised through relations. This opposition is productive, as it makes both knowable: they play off one another as they illuminate and mask the other. This complex relationship Strathern terms a 'merographic connection': domains can be part of something else, but nothing is ever a self-contained whole, as it can only be re-described from another perspective, thereby taking on, however slightly, the character of something else. Nature, in this way of thinking, is particularly significant because it has the capacity to act as a baseline or universal reference point. In contemporary Britain, nature seems also to have become laden with moral authority and ethical potency. For example, we are used to the idea that naturalness is something to be strived for, whether in selecting baby food or assessing beauty. This is of course a particularly middle-class obsession, but we would suggest that this is all the more reason to take it seriously, since, as Strathern also points out, the middle class dominates politics, media and the public sector, so their[2] ideas, including about the ethics of nature, are disproportionately influential in mainstream public discourse.

In *After Nature*, Strathern (1992) predicted that, with increasingly minute interventions into biological processes, from genetics and embryology to pharmacology and agriculture, nature would lose its ability to ground fundamental claims about who we are, how we are related to each other and how we should live. She proposed that exposing the complexities of nature through its technologisation and commodification would cause it to become 'flattened'. Nature would, in other words, lose its ontological and moral purchase. Meanwhile, morality and ethics would become increasingly individualised because of a lack of stable reference points in a world where biotechnology has shaken former certainties.

This special issue responds to Strathern's provocative predictions by considering a diverse range of contemporary relationships to nature over 20 years after her momentous speculations. Nature is undoubtedly a polysemous concept with particular local, individual and contextual meanings, yet despite this elasticity its ability to act as an ultimate reference point seems to have become stronger, rather than weaker. The issue will focus on nature's moral force and examine the connections and disjunctures between nature and ethics across cultural, species, geographic and ethical boundaries. The papers will show that, while nature remains an ambiguous and risky force, we are in a time in which it can still act as an ultimate reference point and boundary-marker, and that it is, vitally, invested with profound ethical authority.

The papers in this collection examine how working directly with the natural world (re)produces specific conceptions of the natural and the ethical, as well as the ways in which people make competing and apparently contradictory claims on and for nature, sometimes within the same or geographically and culturally close locations. They all reflect on how an ethicised nature – that is, a formulation of nature which assumes it has a fundamentally ethical or good character – bears on how people understand themselves, their relations to others (human and non-human) and on the connections between people, as well as the role of a naturalised ethics in structuring relationships between people, the natural world and other living beings (see also Ingold 2000).

The papers in this special issue examine the connections and disjunctures between nature and ethics across cultural, species, geographic and moral boundaries. They provide a comparative perspective on the varied and complex ways in which nature and discourses of naturalness pervade people's lives at all levels, from the intimacies of familial relationships to the production and consumption of food, the gendered division of labour, trans-species relations, discourses of science and truth, perceptions of the landscape and the politics of emotion and identity.

Nature in Anthropological Theory and Ethnography

Our understanding of the concept of nature has evolved alongside anthropology itself. As Hastrup (2013: 1) has written,

> Theoretical advancement in anthropology today is precipitated by new insights into the deep-seated entanglements of natural and social, of human and non-human, and of organic and non-organic forms. Through such entanglements, worlds emerge simultaneously as empirical and analytical objects.

She describes a shift from the work to 'dismantle the dualism' of nature and society done in the 1990s, especially in the work of Descola and Pálsson (1996), towards actually moving 'beyond' the dualism. This attempt to move beyond the nature–culture dichotomy is epitomised by Philippe Descola's recent effort to take a 'Big-Time Thinker' approach to this problem. The aim of *Beyond Nature and Culture*, as stated in the title, is commendable, but we wonder if it is really possible to move beyond any dualism whilst still working within its terms and we remain unconvinced by Descola's proposition that a better understanding of human life lies in tracing collective 'schemas' (see Fitzgerald 2013 for a cogent critique on this and related points). Furthermore, we would add that, in getting caught up in the traffic in nature between ourselves, anthropologists are in danger of losing sight of the ways in which ideas of nature evolve amongst *other* people (i.e. non-anthropologists), with whose ideas we are, after all, supposedly most concerned.

The following review, which is not intended to be an extensive overview of nature as a concept in anthropological theory, but to provide the reader with a refresher of the extensive conversation over the last 25 years, follows three strands of the debates which are most relevant to the papers in this special issue: kinship and gender, environmentalism and human–animal relations. However, it should be clear that debates about nature touch most aspects of anthropological theory and research. Two common problems for social theorists grappling with ideas of nature and the natural are, firstly, the fact that nature is a powerful rhetorical resource for making moral and political claims and secondly, the tenacity of the nature–culture distinction in many folk models, both historical and contemporary.

At the turn of the twentieth century, anthropological references to the 'natural' conveyed a universalising approach to analysing the structure and function of social roles and relationships. This is perhaps most forcefully exemplified by the idea of a universal biological sexual division of labour that relegated women into caring roles at home and reproductive work while men dominated the public sphere of the market and politics. This naturalised division of labour, rooted in fundamental assumptions about the natural nature of sexual reproduction, structured anthropological thinking, so that it seemed plausible to divide social worlds into dichotomous domains of public/private; production/reproduction and work/home. Subsequently, anthropologists, including most notably Schneider (1984) and Collier and Yanagisako (1987), demonstrated that the apparent universality of nature in anthropological analysis and the corresponding social relationships were, in fact, projections of specific Western knowledge practices.

Throughout the 1990s feminist scholars actively deconstructed the relationship between biological universals of sex and gender, elucidating the 'social construction' of biology. Ideas that women, by virtue of biology, were geared and built for roles in the private, domestic and reproductive spheres have been systemically challenged as ethnography showed that these categories and logics do not hold firm across space and time (see, for example, Strathern 1980; Moore 1988). In place of biological sexual difference translating into universal sex categories and roles, gender was no long *a priori*, predictable or fixed, but rather, a symbolically constituted social construction resulting in naturalised difference and inequality (MacCormack & Strathern 1980; Ortner & Whitehead 1981; Moore 1988; Atkinson & Errington 1990). Gender was defined as the 'cultural elaboration of the meaning and significance of the natural facts of biological differences between women and men' (Moore 1999: 149). Collier and Yanagisako (1987) further advanced this deconstructive move by questioning the biological 'facts' of sex. Butler (1990) then showed that biological sex is actually an effect of gender and that gender codes what we take to be the natural basis for differences between men and women.

Parallel to these feminist critiques has been the emergence of the new kinship studies, which have drawn on ethnographic accounts of the fast-moving world of reproductive and other biotechnologies. New kinship studies built on the foundational work of Schneider (1980 [1968]; cf. 1984), which illustrated how the 'order of nature' and 'the order of law' are merged in anthropological kinship thinking. Following on from this, and alongside the feminist critique of biological universals, the idea of 'natural facts' came to be recognised as a specific Western folk model. Strathern (1992) subsequently examined the many definitions of nature and the complex way in which it is implicated in the structure and (re)production of Euro-American and anthropological knowledge practices. This has led to a much-needed examination of the substance and coding of nature, which was previously taken for granted (Franklin & McKinnon 2001).

A key development in anthropological theory in recent decades has been the thorough reconsideration of nature as a variable, contingent category that encompasses many different meanings, not only in the contrasts between Western and non-Western societies (Strathern 1980; Descola & Pálsson 1996), but also within Western societies (Strathern 1992; 2003; James 1993; Tsing 1994; Yanagisako & Delaney 1994; Macnaghten & Urry 1998; Franklin *et al.* 2000; Thompson 2001; 2002; Franklin 2003; Gould 2005; Keller 2008).

Franklin (1997: 57) argues that understanding the idiom of naturalness is essential to grasping Euro-American cultures; this is particularly acute given the close connections that she identifies between anthropologists' own ideas about nature and what they find in their ethnographies of other cultures.

For Yanagisako and Delaney, nature picked up where Christianity left off after the decline of institutionalised religion in western European and North American societies:

> [W]hat was left was a rule-governed Nature, Nature stripped of its cosmological moorings and therefore presumably generalizable to all peoples. Rather than the dichotomy between the natural and supernatural, what was left was 'nature' vs. what man did with it – namely, 'culture'. This move obscured the specificity of the concept of 'nature'. (1994: 4; see also Sahlins 1996)

Through history and in different places, nature has had different forms, meanings and moral valences (see Abram & Lien 2011). But, nature does not only shift because of the vagaries of history – polysemy is an inherent part of its own nature and scholars in anthropology and cultural studies have noted the many meanings that it has in the English language alone (Schneider 1980 [1968]; Williams 1983; Cronon 1996; Franklin 1997: 54; Keller 2008: 118). As Keller (2008) argues, blurring nature's sometimes disparate meanings is an inherent feature of Euro-American thinking about this concept. In the twenty-first century, nature comes clothed in the vestiges of the multiple meanings it has acquired through history. We argue that this ability to encompass multiple meanings is important in giving nature its potency, and that this grows with the increasing meanings it takes on. Nature's specific potency in Euro-American thinking is due to the fact that, amongst its many meanings, it is a grounding or baseline, and thus fundamentally knowable, but *at the same time* a transcendent and cosmological principle that is ultimately unfathomable, not least because of its ever-expanding meanings.

While anthropological attention towards nature has largely emerged from the study of kinship, reproduction and gender, environmentalism, and the meanings that nature has for people concerned about the future of the natural world, has come to receive attention from anthropologists (see Descola & Pálsson 1996; Berglund 1998; Macnaghten & Urry 1998; Dow 2010a; Choy 2011; Milton 1993). This has occurred alongside the environmentalist movement's increasing influence on Western, and to some extent global, politics, economics and culture. Scholars of environmentalism have shown how the contingent meanings of nature may be employed to support particular claims and effect specific aims by those working in this movement and with animals (Yearley 1993; Thompson 2002). Some scientists have also sought to reflect the impact of our deepening awareness of anthropogenic environmental change by labelling our current age as the 'Anthropocene' (see Latour 2013).

Eeva Berglund did fieldwork with environmental activists in various projects in one town in Germany, providing a valuable illustration of the kind of work such activists do and the meanings they place on nature and the natural world. Her ethnography demonstrates that, rather than taking concepts such as science and nature as universal constants in our analysis, they should be treated as contingent categories of thought that are used for particular purposes and with specific effects. As she says, Euro-Americans

> mix and match nature and culture even as we struggle to be consistent in setting boundaries between them. We still act (and agonise) with nature in mind ... it is upon the power that enables the establishing of those boundaries, that anthropologists are able to comment. (1998: 13)

In the UK, at least, what was once called the green movement has been re-conceptualised, and re-marketed, as 'ethical living'. A turn towards conscious reflection on how we live our lives has emerged alongside the increasing currency of environmental thinking in culture and politics (see also Grove-White 1993). As Cronon writes:

> Popular concern about the environment often implicitly appeals to a kind of naïve realism for its intellectual foundation, more or less assuming that we can pretty easily recognize nature when we see it and thereby make uncomplicated choices between natural things, which are good, and unnatural things, which are bad. Much of the moral authority that has made environmentalism so compelling as a popular movement flows from its appeal to nature as a stable external source of non-human values against which human actions can be judged without much ambiguity. (1996: 25–26)

The importance of ideas about nature and the natural world in contemporary life has been particularly successfully demonstrated by anthropological studies of relationships between people and non-human animals. The study of humans' relations with other animals is as old as the discipline, not least because so many early ethnographies were located in communities which relied on hunting and subsistence agriculture to survive and theorists have long paid attention to the symbolism of non-human animals, as in the long-standing debate on totemism. Lévi-Strauss' contribution to this debate was to move it 'toward the intellect' in his suggestion that totemic animals (and plants) are 'good to think' (1962: 89). Particular groups identify themselves with specific animals not because of their economic utility, he said, but their symbolic and metonymic efficacy.

In a review of work on human–animal relations in anthropology, Mullin (1999) notes the relationship between trends in anthropological thinking and the treatment of animals in ethnography. She sees the 'windows and mirrors' approach as a productive one, and makes the related point that, just as ethnographic accounts of Western kinship can help expose some of the underlying assumptions of anthropologists that have informed kinship theory, ethnographic explication of the ways that people think about the other species in their lives similarly reflect the preoccupations of social science. So, an interest in identity politics and reflexivity in the social sciences along with a concurrent increase in the influence of environmentalist discourse has come alongside a mushrooming of attention paid to the relations between people and animals.

As Cassidy (2002: 129) demonstrates in her analysis of human–horse relations in England's Newmarket racing society, animals demonstrate the 'flexibility' of how people use analogical connections in the making of culture (see also Edwards 2000), yet they are not simply passive signifiers of human self-obsession, but dynamic agents. She shows this in the way that ideas about horses both reflect and reproduce ideas about the 'natural order' in Newmarket. As this suggests, animals are not only good to think with, but also good to act with. As Cassidy shows, the animals that human groups identify with may be thought of as family at one moment and an alien species at another and such ideas can inform and reproduce particular ideologies about gender, class and reproduction in humans.

The global call to 'Save the Whale' was one of the earliest examples of environmentalist campaigning and remains metonymic of the movement, so it is a useful illustration of many of the key features of humans' contemporary relations with non-human animals. At the advent of the whaling industry, these marine mammals were largely seen as economic resources to be harvested for profit. Now, although there are of course divergent views within the anti-whaling camps (Stoett 1997: 105; cf. Einarsson 1993), they are popularly seen as hapless victims of the excesses of human industry which we humans have an ethical responsibility to conserve and protect. Writing about anti-whaling views, Peter Stoett states, 'Environmental issues have ethics at their heart: questions of what constitutes proper human behaviour and proper relations between people and nature' (1997: 108). What is particularly interesting about the global Save the Whale campaign is its successful establishment of an *ethical* imperative to protect cetaceans, which has been concurrent with the shift from green politics to ethical living (Dow 2010a, 2010b). As with other strands of the environmentalist movement like organic foods and recycling, this has rested on the association of certain objects *and actions* with nature.

The Anthropology of Ethics

Questions of ethics, morality and the good have come to prominence within anthropology in recent years. As James Laidlaw has put it in his recent book on the anthropology of ethics,

> Everywhere human conduct is pervaded by an ethical dimension – by questions of the rightness and wrongness of actions, of what we owe to each other, of the kind of person we think we are or aspire to be – so it is an inescapable part of what anthropologists study. (2013: 1; see also Lambek 2010; Faubion 2011)

As some of the leading figures of this movement make clear, however, this should not be seen as anthropology suddenly discovering ethics, but more a turning up of the volume on the ethical so that we are more explicit about its ubiquity in everyday social life. Laidlaw (2013: 2) makes a useful parallel with the study of gender in anthropology and expresses the hope that, like gender, ethics will progress from being seen as a discrete subject of enquiry or subdiscipline towards being recognised by the whole discipline as something that pervades all human thought and conduct and so should not be heuristically divorced from the rest of social life or studied only by moral philosophers.

Robbins (2012: para. 4) has sounded a worthwhile note of caution in the recent 'ethical turn' in anthropology by warning that if we are to make the most of it, anthropology 'will need to develop some more sustained intellectual debates and some more established (though not necessarily compatible) theoretical positions that set out central issues a large number of contributors find it useful to address'. One of the strongest arguments of this blossoming body of literature is the point that anthropology is well equipped to study ethical speech and action because of its method and mode of enquiry. Ethnography allows us to capture the ubiquity of ethics in social life, as well as the complex and contingent interactions between social relations, moral edicts, political-economic structures and individual judgements that inform ethical life and self-fashioning.

One of the major points of interest in the development of this field within anthropology in recent years has centred on debates about how and where to locate 'freedom'. Laidlaw (2002; 2013) has made a strong case for abandoning the recently fashionable yet rather strange and contradictory concept of 'agency'. Drawing particularly on Foucault's work on the care of the self, which has been a major influence in the anthropology of ethics, Laidlaw emphasises the point that, while the ethical forms and codes on which ethical subjects can draw are based on their particular cultural and social milieux, they consciously reflect on their choices and actions and this is, for Laidlaw, the action of freedom. Faubion (2011) similarly makes the point that ethical subjects are in a constant process of self-fashioning, taking up shifting subject positions, which must be constantly maintained, while Robbins (2012) has noted the need to take account of both the 'socially given' and the 'idiosyncrasies' which subjects develop as part of their particular projects of self-fashioning.

Lambek (2008; 2010) is similarly influenced by Foucault's work on ethics, though he also draws on Aristotelian virtue ethics, from which he takes the concept of *phronesis*, which he translates as practical judgement. Lambek argues against the concept of freedom in favour of judgement as 'the fulcrum of everyday ethics' (2010: 26). He says that,

> Judgment entails discerning when to follow one's commitments and when to depart from them, or how to evaluate competing or incommensurable commitments; thus a focus on judgment transcends a divide between freedom and obligation, between conventional morality and charismatic innovation, or between performative felicity and subjective sincerity. (2010: 28)

Despite their slightly different takes (and this extends to where, and whether, they draw the line between ethics and morality just as it does to their attitudes to the concept of freedom), what these theorists have in common is the view that ethical life is not constituted by unthinking rule-following, but that subjects have the capacity to step back from themselves and consider what is the good, or best available, thing to do or say in a particular situation. On this note, we would add that another strength that anthropology brings to the ethical table is its attunement to questions of context, which broaden the focus beyond the individual out to her wider environment and interactions with others.

We agree that ethics is an inescapable part of life and that there is much rich material to be found by anthropologists who turn their attention to ethics in everyday life. We also find the attention that has been drawn to 'freedom' and judgement in the establishment of this movement within anthropology to be helpful. Not only do we appreciate a model of human thought and action which leaves room for conscious reflection, but also we believe that this emphasis on the complexity and contingency of ethics and ethical self-fashioning reflects its current interactions with nature, as explored in the papers in this special issue.

Ethnography of Nature and Ethics in the Twenty-First Century

In this special issue, we wish to draw attention to the ways in which ideas of the natural and ethical virtues can both act as grounding concepts for people's decisions, thoughts and actions and to the fact that these concepts often work in conjunction with each other, though not necessarily in predictable ways. We therefore wish to provoke readers to reflect upon the rich, complex and contingent meanings of both nature and ethics, how they interact with each other and how they operate in different contexts. Given the importance of concepts of nature and naturalness in informing boundary-making practices, nature needs to be treated as an ethnographic subject in a way that recognises its ability to shape-shift and to cross human borders whilst still retaining cultural and ethical weight. The papers in this special issue propose some ways of responding to this challenge.

Nature and ethics are about life and death. The papers by Faircloth, Gugganig and Dow all illuminate how people formulate and make sense of the creation stories of living things, while Reed reminds us that our greatest ethical decisions concern the end of life as well as its beginning. In each case, specific ideas about nature, however slippery and polysemous they may be upon closer examination, come to the rescue of people groping for ethical guidance in the face of interventions into the most fundamental biological processes.

While some are more explicit than others, each one of the papers in this issue deals with how we conceptualise and live with time. The social sciences of the last 30 years have been coloured by exhilaration at the pace at which technologies in the natural sciences have been moving, and the challenges that poses for end-users and their wider communities. Each of these papers shows how novelty rubs shoulders with established practice in the ways in which people assimilate and/or reject technological innovations into their everyday lives and ethics. It is hard to know, while in the eye of the storm, whether we really are living in times of unprecedented change, but as social scientists we can at least pay attention to the complex interplay between nostalgic yearnings and hurried acceptance of such developments. Faircloth's article demonstrates the intricacies involved in making claims on nature, human nature and history through the rhetoric of the 'hominid blueprint' for infant feeding, showing just what is at stake in making claims on and with nature. This is further demonstrated by Gugganig's description of the different kinships and natures at stake in the development of genetically engineered taro in Hawai'i.

As work on human–animal relationships has shown, the ways in which people manage the natural, the ethical and the relationship between the two are structured by recognition and identity. Reed demonstrates that working with animals requires a certain 'ontological choreography' (Thompson 2001; see also Thompson 2002) and that detachment from nature and the natural world can enable denaturing or unethical behaviour. His paper shows the shifting moral valence of nature and the different regimes of value at play in how people conceptualise their ethical responsibilities towards the natural world.

Our apprehensions of nature and ethics are about making and sustaining meaning. Furthermore, the rhetorical claims we make with nature are a means through which we can express our ethics and hence identify ourselves as ethical people. Dow makes this point through the example of how people think about surrogacy and maternal bonding. Like Reed, she illustrates the politics of small differences in her analysis of how people conceptualise maternal bonding while showing that, despite these differences, ideas of the natural continue to act as a robust source of ethical guidance. As she and the other authors in this issue show, even in the Western world, morality and ethics have not become atomised acts of individual choice, nor is it true to say that our values have become so 'literalised' (Strathern 1992) or our morality so secularised or individualised, that we are devoid of grounding concepts. Instead, this special issue works from the premise that nature – while an ever-shifting, kaleidoscopic concept – acts as a tenacious and powerful reference point that can provide the basis for moral judgements and ethical decisions, however slippery they appear on closer inspection.

We make sense of the world around us, and the other living beings within it, by drawing lines; marking boundaries facilitates comprehension. Yet, as the comparative project of anthropology suggests, interpretation often entails the crossing of those boundaries. Hastrup has proposed thinking of anthropology's contemporary engagement with nature as 'edgework', by which she means not so much studying edgy or risky practices, as the term has traditionally been used, but instead practising an anthropology that 'resist[s] institutional calculation and conceptual routinization in the interest of exploring new possibilities of being' (2013: 2). This is an anthropology, she argues, that is generative because it works within the oscillations between certainty and uncertainty about how worlds are made and maintained.

NATURE AND ETHICS ACROSS BORDERS

The title of this special issue refers on one level to the geographical scope of the papers within it, which traverse Scotland, England, France and Hawaii, but it also nods to the fact that each paper examines skirmishes along the borders of the natural, demonstrating the different ways in which their transgression can bring us face to face with our ethical and moral values. As Ai Hasegawa's proposal to give birth to a shark demonstrates, we become most aware of borders when we cross them. Snaring animals, long-term breastfeeding, genetic engineering and surrogacy are all practices that cross quotidian borders. They force us to consider our 'fleshy entanglements' (Haraway 2007) with non-human animals, the nature of the things that enter and exit our bodies, the morality of our exploitation of the natural world and ultimately what value, if any, these borders have.

If, in the contemporary Western world, describing something as natural gives it a moral force, demarcating the (un)natural has political consequences. As Reed argues, green politics and animal rights are a powerful riposte to the modernist idea that ultimate power comes from subduing and controlling nature. The ethical decision to live 'closer to nature' can be a way of absolving oneself of the pressure to choose that is the condition of the postmodern subject, or even a means of resisting hegemonic expectations about human motive and action. But, as Dow and Faircloth both show in their discussions of the naturalisation of motherhood, it can also have the (in these cases, unintended) consequence of reproducing normative expectations of gender, kinship and the division of labour.

Ultimately, these ethnographic examples show how people in different places use nature to make claims, preserve hierarchies and formulate identities and it suggests that nature is a concept in rude health in the twenty-first century, even in the context of a new explicitness about choice in natural and biological connections. The papers here describe worlds in which nature is used to demarcate what is ethically (im)possible and to support truth claims in an apparently uncertain postmodern world. They therefore remind us to pay attention to the continued salience of nature in different people's folk models, even as we may seek to move 'beyond' the nature–culture dichotomy in our analyses of human social life. In her afterword, Alana Jelinek discusses her own encounters with nature and ethics and reflects on the ethical actions of relating to Others of any species. From the perspective of artist-informant, she offers some further thoughts about the relations between nature and ethics and points tantalisingly towards the place of politics and religion in these complex connections.

Nature is undoubtedly a polysemous concept with particular local and individual meanings, yet rather than becoming 'flattened', nature seems to retain its ability to act as an ultimate reference point even as is vacillates between multiple meanings. Franklin writes that 'the category of the natural remains central to the production of difference, not only as a shifting classificatory category, but through *processes* of naturalization, de-naturalization, and re-naturalization' (2003: 68, original emphasis). She argues, therefore, for an analytical approach that considers the 'traffic in nature' (Franklin *et al.* 2000). As she says, a key feature of Euro-American ideas about kinship, biology and nature is their ability to encompass, and thus constantly vacillate between, 'given' and 'made' elements of knowledge. Nature may have come to seem more fluid, but instead of weakening it, this ability to shape-shift has in fact strengthened it (Franklin 2003: 68; see also Franklin 2014). The papers in this special issue demonstrate that it is nature's ability to take on different, overlapping forms that gives it continued power. They show that, while nature seems to many theorists to be at ontological risk from human activities and technology, it can still act as an ultimate reference point and as an ethical guide in a time that has also been described as one of rapid cultural, technological and moral change.

Acknowledgements
We wish to thank all of the participants at the panel at the American Anthropological Association Annual Meeting in 2011 that laid the foundations for this special issue, including especially the discussants, Sarah Franklin and Michal Nahman, for their invaluable reflections. We are very grateful to Mark Graham at *Ethnos* for guiding us through publication and for the feedback of numerous anonymous reviewers. We are also grateful to Ai Hasegawa for letting us include a photo of her work.

Disclosure statement
No potential conflict of interest was reported by the authors.

Notes
1. While Hasegawa states the world population (in 2012) was nine billion, it is in fact 7.2 billion as of early 2014.
2. Perhaps we should say here, 'our ideas', since both authors are also part of this British middle-class milieu.

References
Abram, Simone & Marianne Elisabeth Lien. 2011. Performing Nature at World's Ends. *Ethnos: Journal of Anthropology*, 76(1):3–18.

Atkinson, J. & S. Errington (eds.). 1990. *Power and Difference: Gender in Island Southeast Asia.* Stanford, CA: Stanford University Press.

Berglund, Eeva K. 1998. *Knowing Nature, Knowing Science: An Ethnography of Environmental Activism.* Cambridge: The White Horse Press.

Butler, Judith. 1990. *Gender Trouble: Feminism and the Subversion of Identity.* London: Routledge.

Cassidy, Rebecca. 2002. *The Sport of Kings: Kinship, Class and Thoroughbred Breeding in Newmarket.* Cambridge: Cambridge University Press.

Choy, Tim. 2011. *Ecologies of Comparison: An Ethnography of Endangerment in Hong Kong.* Durham, NC: Duke University Press.

Collier, Jane F. & Sylvia J. Yanagisako. 1987. *Gender and Kinship: Essays Toward a Unified Analysis.* Stanford, CA: Stanford University Press.

Cronon, William. (ed). 1996. *Uncommon Ground: Rethinking the Human Place in Nature.* London: W. & W. Norton.

Descola, Philippe, & Gísli Pálsson. 1996. *Nature and Society: Anthropological Perspectives.* London: Routledge.

Dow, Katharine. 2010a. *A Stable Environment: Surrogacy and the Good Life in Scotland* (Ph.D. thesis), The London School of Economics and Political Science (LSE).

——. 2010b, September. Stories from the Field: The Sperm Whale's Teeth. *Anthropology Now*, 2(2):63–69.

Edwards, Jeanette. 2000. *Born and Bred: Idioms of Kinship and New Reproductive Technologies in England.* Oxford: Oxford University Press.

Einarsson, Niels. 1993. All Animals are Equal But Some are Cetaceans: Conservation and Culture Conflict. In *Environmentalism: The View from Anthropology*, edited by Kay Milton. pp. 73–84. London: Routledge.

Faubion, James D. 2011. *An Anthropology of Ethics.* Cambridge: Cambridge University Press.

Fitzgerald, Des. 2013, October 11. Philippe Descola's *Beyond Nature and Culture. Somatosphere.* http://somatosphere.net/2013/10/philippe-descolas-beyond-nature-and-culture.html

Franklin, Sarah. 1997. *Embodied Progress: A Cultural Account of Assisted Conception.* London: Routledge.

——. 2003. Re-thinking Nature–culture: Anthropology and the New Genetics. *Anthropological Theory*, 3(1):65–85.

——. 2014. Analogic Return: The Reproductive Life of Conceptuality. *Theory, Culture & Society*, 31:243–261.

Franklin, Sarah & Susan McKinnon (eds.). 2001. *Relative Values: Reconfiguring Kinship Studies.* Durham, NC: Duke University Press.

Franklin, Sarah, Jackie Stacey & Celia Lury. 2000. *Global Nature, Global Culture.* London: Sage.

Gould, Rebecca Kneale. 2005. *At Home in Nature: Modern Homesteading and Spiritual Practice in America.* London: University of California Press.

Grove-White, Robin. 1993. Environmentalism: A New Moral Discourse for Technological Society? In *Environmentalism: The View from Anthropology*, edited by Kay Milton. pp. 18–30. London: Routledge.

Haraway, Donna J. 2007. *When Species Meet.* Minneapolis: University of Minnesota Press.

Hasegawa, Ai. 2012. 'I Wanna Deliver a Shark...' *Design for the Real World*, Royal College of Art, London. See: http://aihasegawa.info/

Hastrup, Kirsten. 2013. Nature: Anthropology on the Edge. In *Anthropology and Nature*, edited by Kirsten Hastrup. pp. 1–26. London: Routledge.

Ingold, Tim. 2000. *The Perception of the Environment: Essays on Livelihood, Dwelling and Skill*. London: Routledge.

James, Allison. 1993. Eating Green(s): Discourses of Organic Food. In *Environmentalism: The View from Anthropology*, edited by Kay Milton. pp. 205–218. London: Routledge.

Keller, Evelyn Fox. 2008. Nature and the Natural. *BioSocieties*, 3:117–124.

Laidlaw, James. 2002. For an Anthropology of Ethics and Freedom. *Journal of the Royal Anthropological Institute*, 8(2):311–332.

——. 2013. *The Subject of Virtue: An Anthropology of Ethics and Freedom*. Cambridge: Cambridge University Press.

Lambek, M. 2008. Value and Virtue. *Anthropological Theory*, 8(2): 133–157.

Lambek, Michael (ed.). 2010. *Ordinary Ethics: Anthropology, Language, and Action*. New York: Fordham University Press.

Latour, Bruno. 2013, February 18–28. *Facing Gaia: Six Lectures on the Political Theology of Nature*. Being the Gifford Lectures on Natural Religion, Edinburgh.

Lévi-Strauss, Claude. 1962. *Totemism* [Rodney Needham Trans.]. London: Merlin Press.

MacCormack, Carol & Marilyn Strathern. 1980. *Nature, Culture and Gender*. Cambridge: Cambridge University Press.

Macnaghten, Phil & John Urry. 1998. *Contested Natures*. London: Sage Publications.

Milton, Kay. 1993. Introduction: Environmentalism and Anthropology. In *Environmentalism: The View from Anthropology*, edited by Kay Milton. pp. 1–17. London: Routledge.

Moore, Henrietta L. 1988. *Feminism and Anthropology*. Cambridge: Polity Press.

—— (ed.). 1999. *Anthropological Theory Today*. Cambridge: Polity Press.

Mullin, Molly H. 1999. Mirrors and Windows: Sociocultural Studies of Human-Animal Relationships. *Annual Review of Anthropology*, 28:201–224.

Ortner, Sherry B. & Harriet Whitehead. 1981. *Sexual Meanings: The Cultural Construction of Gender and Sexuality*. Cambridge: Cambridge University Press.

Robbins, Joel. 2012. On Becoming Ethical Subjects: Freedom, Constraint, and the Anthropology of Morality. *Anthropology of this Century*, Issue 5. http://aotcpress.com/articles/ethical-subjects-freedom-constraint-anthropology-morality/

Sahlins, Marshall. 1996. The Sadness of Sweetness: The Native Anthropology of Western Cosmology. *Current Anthropology*, 37:395–415.

Schneider, David M. 1980 [1968]. *American Kinship: A Cultural Account* (2nd ed.). London: University of Chicago Press.

—— 1984. *A Critique of the Study of Kinship*. Ann Arbor: University of Michigan Press.

Stoett, Peter J. 1997. *The International Politics of Whaling*. Vancouver: UBC Press.

Strathern, Marilyn. 1980. No Nature, No Culture: The Hagen Case. In *Nature, Culture and Gender*, edited by Carol MacCormack and Marilyn Strathern. pp. 174–222. Cambridge: Cambridge University Press.

——. 1992. *After Nature: English Kinship in the Late Twentieth Century*. Cambridge: Cambridge University Press.

——. 2003. Still Giving Nature a Helping Hand? Surrogacy: A Debate about Technology and Society. In *Surrogate Motherhood: International Perspectives*, edited by Rachel Cook and Shelley Day Sclater with Felicity Kaganas. pp. 281–296. Oxford: Hart Publishing.

Thompson, Charis. 2001. Strategic Naturalizing: Kinship in an Infertility Clinic. In *Relative Values: reconfiguring kinship studies*, edited by S. Franklin and S. McKinnon. pp. 175–222. Durham, NC: Duke University Press.

——. 2002. When Elephants Stand for Competing Models of Nature. In *Complexities: Social Studies of Knowledge Practices*, edited by Annemarie Mol & John Law. pp. 166–190. Durham, NC: Duke University Press.

Tsing, Anna Lowenhaupt. 1994. Empowering Nature, or: Some Gleanings in Bee Culture. In *Naturalizing Power: Essays in Feminist Cultural Analysis*, edited by Carol Delaney & Sylvia Yanagisako. pp. 113–144. New York: Routledge.

Williams, Raymond. 1983. *Keywords: A Vocabulary of Culture and Society*. London: Fontana Paperbacks.

Yanagisako, Sylvia and Carol Delaney (eds). 1994. *Naturalizing Power: Essays in Feminist Cultural Analysis*. New York: Routledge.

Yearley, Steven. 1993. Standing in for Nature: The Practicalities of Environmental Organisations' Use of Science. In *Environmentalism: The View from Anthropology*, edited by Kay Milton. pp. 59–72. London: Routledge.

'Natural' Breastfeeding in Comparative Perspective: Feminism, Morality, and Adaptive Accountability

Charlotte Faircloth

ABSTRACT *Based on research in London and Paris with mothers from an international breastfeeding support organisation, this paper explores the narratives of women who breastfeed their children 'to full term' (typically for a period of several years) as part of a philosophy of 'attachment parenting'. In line with wider cultural trends (in the UK, at least), one of the most prominent 'accountability strategies' used by this group of mothers to explain their full-term breastfeeding is the claim that this is 'most natural', drawing on an evolutionary 'hominid blueprint' of care, as well as an ecological perspective on social life more broadly. What follows in the paper is a reflection on how notions of 'natural' parenting are given credence in narratives of mothering, and how this is used adaptively in local contexts as part of women's 'identity work'. If in the UK the 'natural' is used as a moral grounding for action, the same cannot be said for women in France. Using a comparative perspective, the argument is that this reflects very different trajectories within the feminist movement in the UK and France. Where in certain mileux in the UK it is considered desirable, even mandatory, to 'get in touch with' nature, in France, it is considered something to escape, subordinate, and resist. Far from being 'flattened', then, the purchase of nature as it relates to moral negotiations of mothering appears to be stronger than ever.[1]*

What anthropologists say: Determining what is a natural age of weaning for human beings raises some problems. Human beings' ideas about when and how to wean are often determined by culture, not necessarily by what is best or natural for babies and mothers. Anthropologists who have studied weaning have found a great variety in weaning ages, from birth (in much of the United States and Western society in general) to age seven or eight in other cultures.... Dr Dettwyler has used the example of primates to try to determine a natural weaning age for humans, since 'gorillas and chimpanzees share more than ninety-eight percent of their genes with humans' but are lacking the cultural biases of humans. (D. Bengson, *How Weaning Happens*, emphasis added)

This paper explores the accounts of women in London and Paris who breastfeed their children to 'full term' (as known as 'extended' or 'long-term' breastfeeding). Breastfeeding 'until their child outgrows the need' – which ranged between one and eight years old, but was typically for three or four years in this study – was spoken about in both settings as part of a 'natural' trajectory, doing justice to what is termed a 'hominid blueprint' for behaviour. As in the quote above, this blueprint is derived from archaeological and anthropological evidence; in some cases, through historical studies of our evolutionary past, in others, through recourse to contemporary primates or 'primitive' peoples who are understood to represent it today. Drawing on this evolutionary paradigm as well as psychological work on attachment and an ecological world view, full-term breastfeeding is typically practised as part of an 'attachment parenting' philosophy (Bobel 2002; Faircloth 2013).

The operation of the natural as a domain of foundational cultural practice has long been a site of anthropological interest (e.g. MacCormack and Strathern 1980), and since then, there has been a move towards foregrounding the 'constitutive role of metaphor, analogy, classification, narrative, and genealogy in the production of natural facts' (Franklin 1990: 127, see introduction to this special issue). It should be said at the outset, therefore, that the intention here is not to explore whether these mothers correctly rehearse discussions going on within (both biological and social) anthropological disciplines around the evolutionary bases of human mothering. In using the term 'nature' to produce models of mothering, the mothers here draw on elements of academic discussions that support their overall philosophy, but tend to overlook aspects that do not (such as those which stress flexibility, in place of the need to breastfeed for a specific length of time). Rather, the intention is to explore the implications of this construction of 'natural' mothering in particular social, economic, and political circumstances. The broad spectrum of anthropological perspectives on this issue converges on flexibility and adaptation to local circumstances as the most prominent features of infant care; and that *includes* adaption to local cultural values, foregrounded in the British and French contexts here.

In the two case studies (London and Paris), women's narratives about 'natural' parenting draw on a set anthropologically informed parenting advice literature. This literature, typically written in the USA, has an increasingly globalised, online reach (albeit with a different reception in each cultural setting). Indeed, this literature rubs up against important, and contrasting, views of nature in British and French cultures, which are also influenced by (and influence) trends in feminism and family policy. If in the UK the 'natural' is used as a moral grounding for action by these mothers, the same cannot be said for women in France. Where in the UK it is considered desirable, even mandatory, to 'get in touch with' nature, in France, 'nature' is considered something to escape, subordinate, and resist. The argument is that while the endorsement of full-term breastfeeding by women in London is a magnification of a culture which encourages intensive, embodied 'natural' parenting on the part of mothers, the same mothering practices look very different in Paris. In French culture, where maternal–infant separation and autonomy is lauded as ideal, embodied care on the part of the mother is perceived as an impingement on female liberty (Badinter 2010).

Context: Parenting Culture and Feeding Practices

Across space and time, societies have had different ideas about children, which in turn shape how parents are expected to behave towards them (Badinter 1980; Fildes 1986; Thurer 1994). Today, in Britain and France, childcare can be roughly divided into styles that are structured, and those that are more liberal. The former is characterised by practices such as scheduled feeds, formula feeding, and separate sleeping. Liberal models, by contrast, take a less regimented approach in favour of more relaxed styles of care, often characterised by practices such as long-term, on-cue breastfeeding, a family bed and 'positive' discipline (Buskens 2001: 75).[2]

Liberal models of childcare have been made most famous by the work of William and Martha Sears who coined the term 'Attachment Parenting' in *The Baby Book* (2003 [1992]). They drew on the work on bonding done by Bowlby and others to argue that the optimum way of caring for a child was to keep mother and baby in prolonged physical contact. The argument is that babies have evolutionary expectations that must be met if they are to mature into happy, healthy children and adults (paraphrased from Bobel 2002: 61). Arguing that modern culture has impeded 'common sense parenting', the Sears say that it is 'what we would all do if left to our own healthy resources' (Sears & Sears 1993: 2):

THE ABC'S OF ATTACHMENT PARENTING (Sears & Sears 2001: 4)
When you practise the Baby B's of AP, your child has a greater chance of growing up with the qualities of the A's and C's:

A's	B's	C's
Accomplished	Birth bonding	Caring
Adaptable	Breastfeeding	Communicative
Adept	Babywearing	Compassionate
Admirable	Bedding close to baby	Confident
Affectionate	Belief in baby's cry	Connected
Anchored	Balance and boundaries	Cuddly
Assured	Beware of baby trainers	Curious

Of course, the distinction between the various models of parenting may be more heuristic than descriptive, as many parents will attest as there may be a gap between intention and outcome (formula feeding not always being a deliberate, reflexive choice, but a necessary intervention if breastfeeding is problematic). But because the plurality exists, at a heuristic level at least, parents are *accountable* for the choice they make both within and between these competing models.

It is also important to note a nominative slippage here. Attachment parenting, as a specific way of raising children, has little correlation with Bowlby's attachment theory: practices such as co-sleeping, breastfeeding and baby wearing are not necessarily tied to the development of greater attachment in mother–infant pairs (see Faircloth 2014 for more on this).[3]

Using Goffman's idea of (1959) 'identity work' – in this case, the narrative processes of self-making that mothers engage in as they account for their parenting practices – is part of an argument that for certain middle-class parents in the London (and to a lesser extent in Paris), the word 'parent' has shifted in recent years from a noun denoting a relationship with a child (something you *are*), to a verb (something you *do*). 'Parenting' is now an occupation in which adults (particularly mothers) are expected to be emotionally absorbed and become personally fulfilled; it is also a growing site of interest to policymakers in the UK, understood as the cause of, and solution to a wide range of social ills (Lee *et al.* 2014). The 'ideal' parenting promoted by these policymakers is financially, physically and emotionally 'intensive', and parents are encouraged to spend a large amount of time, energy and money in raising their children – the 'attachment' parenting explored here just one of many permutations of this (Hays 1996). One of the reasons this injunction wields such power, Hays suggests, is because 'intensive' mothering is perceived as 'the last best defence against what many people see as the impoverishment of social ties, communal obligations, and unremunerated commitments' (1996: xiii).

Feeding, one of the most conspicuously moralised elements of mothering, was the focus of the study. Because of its vital importance for the survival and healthy development of infants, feeding is a highly scrutinised domain where mothers must counter any charges of practising unusual, harmful or morally suspect feeding techniques (Murphy 1999). Powerful feelings about feeding are derived from the fact that it operates as a 'signal issue' which boxes women off into different parenting 'camps' (Kukla 2005).

The World Health Organization (WHO) states that breastfeeding in developed countries should be exclusive for six months and continue 'for up to two years, or beyond' in conjunction with other foods (2003). Along with other EU member states, this is endorsed by both the UK and French governments. Breastfeeding initiation rates at the time of research stood at 78% and 69% in Britain and France, respectively,[4] with no formal statistics existing in either place for rates of breastfeeding at a year, or beyond. While there were no statistics for the number of children breastfed beyond a year in the UK, by six months, 75% of children were totally weaned off breastmilk and only 2% of women breastfed exclusively for the recommended six months (Department of Health 2005a, 2005b).

The women profiled here therefore use various 'accountability strategies', to explain and justify their non-conventional feeding patterns (Faircloth 2013). These centre around referring to what they do as 'most natural' – whether evolutionarily, through recourse to what 'science' says is best, or what 'feels right', and it is the first of these that forms the subject of this paper. At the level of their own 'identity work', women mobilise the moral authority of the natural, to explain, justify and account for their statistically unusual practices. As Cronon notes, the attraction of nature 'for those who wish to ground their moral vision in external reality is its capacity to take disputed values and make them seem innate, essential, eternal, and non-negotiable' (1996: 36). What is interesting, then, is the specific cultural form that the formulation of 'nature' takes, as part of mothers' adaptation to their local environments. What we see is that a (seemingly) scientific, or scholarly justification of a 'natural' style of parenting, drawing on these evolutionary rationales, represents a socially robust kind of knowledge claim for mothers in both settings, albeit with different outcomes explored below (see Faircloth 2013 for more on this).

Methods

The research for this study involved long-term ethnographic fieldwork with women in *La Leche League International* (LLLI) groups, the world's foremost breastfeeding support organisation. The group was founded in 1956 in the USA to support all women who wanted to breastfeed their babies. It is the only group of this kind to have a specific philosophy behind its approach, best summarised as 'mothering through breastfeeding', an approach to parenting at the liberal end of the spectrum described above. Thus, while it offers encouragement for all women who want to breastfeed, it is known among the various breastfeeding support groups to be supportive of women who breastfeed for 'extended' periods, and has a significant proportion of members who practise 'attachment' parenting.

During 2006, and over the course of 8 months in London and 4 months in Paris, I attended 18 local LLLI groups (10 in London, 8 in Paris, including an Anglophone group) complementing this observational data with semi-structured interviews and, later, questionnaires with individual women recruited through these groups across the two cities.

LLL groups run on a four-month cycle, identical the world over addressing various aspects of the breastfeeding experience. The meetings, generally held in a member's home, typically had between 5 and 20 mothers in attendance, with children ranging from newborn to 7 years old (the majority in the younger half of this spectrum).

After I had been attending a group for some time, I asked mothers there if they would be interested in talking to me more formally. Fewer than 900 members of La Leche League Great Britain (LLLGB) were 'paid-up' at the time of research, although nearly 8000 women attended meetings in 2007, according to the 2008 report (LLLI 2008. This is compared with 2500 paying members in France; statistics about the numbers of users were not available.) Thus, I did not make a distinction between those who were paid-up 'members' of LLL and those who were simply 'attendees' (one does not need to be a member to attend meetings, though many mothers do sign up to support their local group if they come regularly).

I interviewed 26 mothers and 13 LLL leaders about their philosophy of parenting and experiences of breastfeeding. In these discussions, I was allowed to go beyond immediate horizons I encountered in the meetings – a particularly important opportunity for a researcher of a topic such as motherhood. Indeed, a formal LLL system was in place, designed to keep the subject of the meeting on breastfeeding itself. Interviews were therefore a time for women to speak more openly about those parts of the philosophy they endorsed, rejected, or otherwise.

I also conducted an email survey, drawn up on the basis of the findings of the interviews, with 25 women in London and 23 in Paris (some of this number included women who were also interviewed, thus the total sample size was 73). The survey explored women's feeding decisions, asking if they felt under pressure to conform to certain social norms, and how their feeding decisions had affected the rest of their lives (such as relationships with friends, family, or health professionals).

In both cases, mothers were in the vast majority white, aged around 34 years old, educated to university level or equivalent and married. More women in the Parisian sample than in the London sample were working full-time, as I discuss further below. Those who identified as 'attachment mothers' made up just over half of the sample in London, and just over a third in Paris. These women were breastfeeding 'to full-term' as part of an 'attachment parenting' philosophy, in addition to being attendees of LLL. The definition of full-term breastfeeding, following LLL convention, was taken to be breastfeeding beyond one year (appreciating that one can feed 'to term' long after this point).

Not all women undertake all of these elements of the attachment parenting philosophy discussed here with the same intensity (such as baby wearing in a sling, or a more ecological approach to illness, for example), but there is certainly cohesion around these sets of values. My classification is based on statistics and responses derived from the questionnaire – that is, from women breastfeeding their children beyond a year – as well as my own observations at group meetings and interviews. (In some cases, women who breastfed beyond one year were not classified as 'attachment' because they did not also ascribe to other elements of the attachment parenting philosophy.)

Certainly not all mothers in the organisation breastfeed to full term, though I engage particularly with the accounts of those who do and with the values they promote and enact. In taking their feeding practices to one end of the spectrum, they magnify mainstream issues around motherhood and 'identity work' in each of the contexts profiled. These accounts do not represent official LLLI philosophy, but are rather particular women's understandings of their parenting experiences.

'Natural' Parenting: Accounts of Ecology and Evolution

A rhetoric of the 'natural' is a major accountability strategy in women's narratives of attachment parenting and full-term breastfeeding, in both London and Paris (although I begin with the London data here before turning to the Parisian comparison below). Ivana and Megan are quoted at length because their answers encompass many of the themes articulated by others:

Charlotte: Can you give me three reasons why you wanted to breastfeed, and why you are still breastfeeding?

Ivana [*Leader applicant, 38, breastfeeding her 3-year-old daughter, emphasis added, London*]: Only three?... we always discuss this sort of thing. I think there are *social* reasons, *health* reasons – physical, emotional, psychological... and the third one, *political* reasons I guess. On a physical health reason, there are a lot of things that are good for the baby and the mother.... [To not use] what is given for free, for the best possible nourishment in so many levels, it is almost like a wasting of a resource... wasting the gift, wasting the opportunities... *I think it is a bit arrogant towards nature*. It is also linked to the political level.... Not supporting the world, the planet, the earth... just something you can exploit for your benefit and discard.

Megan [*41, breastfeeding her 4-year-old son, emphasis added, London*]: You see, the thing is, Charlotte, what I'm doing *is* normal – you know, it's actually *the most natural thing in the world* when you think about it. Children have a *need* for their mother's milk until the age of six, and mothers are designed to fulfil that need. *It feels right, because it's part of our evolution.* The benefits are in the literature. The people who have a problem with it just don't realise what they're saying... *In lots of tribal societies women breastfeed for this long*, and it's just not an issue for them.

Fashions in parenting are best understood as barometers of wider cultural trends, which, in the UK at least, have recently seen a growing validation of the 'natural' way to do things as diverse as eating, learning and treating illness (as the papers in this issue explore). As we see in these accounts, then, at least two kinds of nature emerge – both 'ecological' and 'evolutionary' (the two are, of course, not mutually exclusive; see Faircloth 2013).

Ecological Parenting

As Ivana suggests, full-term breastfeeding is only one choice women in this sample make in cultivating an 'ecological' lifestyle. They often favoured the rhythm method of contraception over pills or intrauterine devices, which were understood to disrupt the body's natural state. When they had their period, they did not use tampons or sanitary towels but a 'menstrual cup', which was more environmentally friendly. At birth, they would eschew 'interventions' and avoid painkillers where possible. Women often used cloth nappies for their children, which were said to be better for the environment (though some women countered that the detergents used to wash them were just as harmful). Children were not necessarily vaccinated, and medical treatments for illness, such as antibiotics, were used only as a last resort, as they were held to interrupt the body's own homeostasis. The family would eat primarily organic, locally grown, whole foods if they could. They abstained from wearing synthetic or branded clothes whenever possible. They recycled. They preferred cycling to driving, and making their own food rather than buying it. As Bobel puts it (writing about the USA), 'natural mothers' resist culture to embrace (a cultural construction of) nature in almost all areas of their lives (2002: 125). And yet – as the nappy example shows – 'natural' is a concept around which strong feelings can coalesce, but actual practices remain unspecified. Indeed, it is the elasticity of the concept – the stretching and contracting to be at once normal, right, non-artificial, traditional, instinctive – that makes it so powerful in women's accountability strategies, and so fundamental to their identity work.

For many attachment mothers I interviewed, resisting nature – by not breastfeeding, for example – is dangerous. Ivana sees it as being 'arrogant' towards nature. Modern culture is seen to be eroding humanity's proper place on the planet. Certainly, the use of nature to advocate particular forms of behaviour is nothing new – as Hume (2000) observed, nature has long served as a moral grounding for action, neatly conflating the 'is' and the 'ought'. Moscucci (2003) notes, using the example of the 'natural' childbirth movement in the UK, that the moral purchase of 'nature' has long served as a political and cultural critique, aimed at the various crises of modern society – be they industrialisation, capitalism, materialism, or urbanisation. The solution to these problems is seen to lie in a return to nature, variously understood as the rural, the primitive, the spiritual or the instinctive (Moscucci 2003). Yet, as these accounts show, 'looking to nature', as a trend that has become particularly prominent in recent years, particularly in UK policy, and is worthy of a closer look. Breastfeeding is regularly promoted as the 'ecological' option which 'leaves no footprint', for example, (Breastfeeding Manifesto Coalition 2007).

Evolutionary Parenting

To argue that human beings do not have evolutionary adaptations or expectations (e.g. of food to eat), or that these are not particularly acute in infancy, would of course be foolish. What is of interest here is the point at which evolutionary 'expectations' become injunctions (often enshrined in policy, or mobilised by advocates of attachment parenting to promote or defend their mothering practices).

It is typical to hear attachment mothers in London, such as Megan, account for the decision to breastfeed to full term in the language of evolutionary adaptation and development. In lay terms, the idea is that women should breastfeed the way primates and 'primitive' humans did (or do), since our bodies adapted to a specific form of lactation because it was evolutionarily advantageous (Hausman 2003). Mothers frequently cited the (US-based) biological anthropologist, and advocate of attachment parenting, Katherine Dettwyler when they used this particular accountability strategy. She uses cross-cultural, cross-species and cross-temporal examples of a range of factors, including age of eruption of first molar and length of gestation, to come to a blueprint for human weaning, free of 'culture'. Dettwyler concludes:

> [I]f humans weaned their offspring according to the primate pattern without regard to beliefs and customs, most children would be weaned somewhere between 2.5 and 7 years of age. (1995: 66)

In Dettwyler's narrative, 'nature' is something monolithic, distinct, unsullied by culture and best represented by primates living 'in the wild' (Bobel 2002: 127). But as Hausman (2003) notes, that humans could ever be culture-free is quite a startling assertion for an anthropologist to make, even in the name of an exercise.

A cross-species blueprint for the time of weaning assumes no interaction between animal and environment – or culture – which, as many primatologists will argue, is not, and has never been, the case: 'Primate infant nutrition is strongly influenced by the ecological and social environment, generating the hypothesis that *flexibility characterising the process is adaptive*, allowing individual organisms to improve the fit between themselves and their local environment' (Wells 2006: 45, emphasis added). In other words, while some primates *might* wean their offspring at a very late age where suitable weaning foods do not exist, this is not necessarily the case where resources are more bountiful. Indeed, where weaning foods are readily available, primate behaviour is characterised by decreased length of lactation to enable the mother to invest her labours in gestating and nurturing other offspring. Furthermore, active weaning behaviour is a feature common to almost all mammals (Wells 2006).

Hrdy (2009) makes the related argument that humans are unique among the apes in their mothering, as cooperative breeders requiring the help of other members of the group to mother successfully. Without such help, they may become destructive of their offspring. Furthermore, she argues that this adaptation is possibly the basis of empathy and language, two of our most human characteristics, making humans even *less* likely to fit a general primate or hominid blueprint. This strongly supports the importance of social context and variability (as emphasised by Hewlett and Lamb's work on foragers living in different environments, 2005).

Yet, the idea that humans essentially have the same body today as they did 400,000 years ago is, for many advocates, a way to rationalise 'full-term' breastfeeding. The environmental conditions under which early humans lived shaped their physiology and their biosocial practices: danger from predators (meaning a need to have infants close at hand so as to stifle any loud cry, usually by nursing); a lack of appropriate weaning foods (meaning prolonged breastfeeding); and a continuous cycle of pregnancy and lactation for fertile females, during which prolonged lactation helped to space childbirth at optimal intervals for infant survival (paraphrased from Hausman 2003: 128).

Mapping this blueprint onto contemporary circumstances means our biology has become a problem. According to attachment mothers in London, norms of modern infant care such as scheduled sleeping and feeding routines are 'out of sync' with the evolutionary requirements of human beings. Thus, part of the appeal of attachment mothering is that the model is imitative of infant care practices following an ancestral pattern that is biologically appropriate to the human species – that is, not only traditional, but *adaptive* in a biological sense (Hausman 2003: 124–125). This is a very powerful notion: 'The idea that specific, supposedly traditional, mothering practices are really evolutionary adaptations – rather than cultural constructions that emerge at a specific historical juncture – is a persuasive rhetoric, delineating natural and unnatural maternal practices within a speculative evolutionary paradigm' (Hausman 2003: 125). Child-led weaning is presented by advocates as 'natural', whereas mother-led weaning is 'cultural' and therefore not appropriately biological (Hausman 2003: 125).

Typically, contemporary foraging societies are used by mothers (or the academics whom they cite) as stand-ins for earlier hominid hunter–gatherers to represent 'natural' patterns of lactation and care, and statistics on length and frequency of lactation among them are used to demonstrate the ancestral pattern.[5] Yet, using the example of the !Kung (an anthropological favourite – see Shostak 2000), Hrdy has provided a critique of evolutionary theory and references to hunter-gatherers as used in the context of contemporary infant care. She argues that while the 'Environment of Evolutionary Adaptedness' – the millions of years during which today's humans' behavioural equipment would have evolved – is a useful theory, it has been sidelined to refer only to the Pleistocene period [see Hausman (2003: 143) for an account of this]. Since most people assume that modern humans were, at one point, hunters on the African savannas, the !Kung of the Kalahari come to represent all hunter-gatherer peoples, and therefore, all peoples (Hewlett and Lamb's work also demonstrates the considerable *variability* among foragers in different environments, 2005). This assumes a constancy of resources over time and space for all humans: '[The] extended half-decade of physical closeness between a mother and her infant [supposedly typified by the !Kung] ... tells us more about the harshness of local conditions and the mothers' lack of safe alternatives than the "natural state" of *all* Pleistocene mothers' (Hrdy 1999: 100-101). Local cultural traditions are largely ignored, and the !Kung are treated as passively representative of human biological patterns. They do not therefore act to create a culture of their own (the idea is that they *do not* have culture); rather, they stand in a vacuum (Hausman 2003: 143).

The attachment mothers (or rather, the authors they cited) in London used 'the primitive' as a site for playing out fantasies of the natural: that !Kung wean their children by pasting bitter herbs onto their breasts (Small 1998: 82), or that they use enemas on their infants, both of which would likely be considered dangerous by many parents, is overlooked. A set of 'cultural blinkers' operates in these attempts to emulate and explain extended periods of lactation (Buskens 2001), meaning evidence which points to variability is often ignored.

The mothers I spoke with do not actually want the hunter-gatherer lifestyle, of course; rather, they cherry-pick those elements which fit with their sensibilities, or, cultural contexts (as we all, ultimately, do). These mothers do not reject all forms of 'culture' – they retain the Internet, for example – but cultivate particular elements of 'nature' as part of the identity work that validates their mothering. To assume that, given the real possibility, !Kung mothers would not also use painkillers in childbirth or formula milk for weaning is to ignore the evidence of numerous other societies. As soon as agriculture made soft weaning foods more available, weaning occurred earlier and babies were spaced more closely together (Maher 1992; Palmer 1993; Hrdy 1999: 201–202).[6]

It is one thing, then, for a !Kung mother living where suitable weaning foods do not exist to breastfeed her four-year-old, and quite another for a woman living in London – and neither of them is more 'natural' than the other. A view of culture as something external to nature presents a dichotomy in which human interaction with, and manipulation of, the environment is considered artificial. Arguably, this adaptation – finding the best fit, including to cultural values – is what evolution has always been about.

[Section moved to end]

A Cross-Cultural Perspective: Paris

While the discourses and practices of parenting may be seen as culturally and historically specific, much recent work has explored how they are currently acquiring a global significance (Faircloth, Hoffman and Layne 2013). Taking this perspective is instructive because the interactions of globally circulating discourses, and constructions of parenting with localised constructs, reveal assumptions and tensions within parenting that enhance our practical and theoretical understanding of the phenomenon. It also allows us to challenge ideas about the moral valence of particular notions of parenting, as well as revealing the many ways in which kinship, identity, and cultural ideals concerning motherhood/fatherhood challenge and resist certain formations of parenting.

Contexts

At the time of research, in the UK, a woman could typically expect 26 weeks (six months) of paid maternity leave with five weeks' additional unpaid leave if desired. (Women were not paid at full rate – it was calculated at 90% for the initial six weeks and then at a flat rate, approximately 33% of average wage, for 20 weeks).[7] In Paris, women could take 16 weeks of (fully) paid leave, then being eligible for longer periods of unpaid leave. Since this is generally split on a 4-week/12-week basis pre- and post-birth, women are expected to return to work when their children are between 10 weeks and 3 months old.[8] In the UK, this point would typically be between five and six months. Paternity leave at the time of research in both countries was two weeks, with only 25% of this time paid in the UK.

Crucially, however, and unlike the UK, France has a system of heavily subsidised, easily available, affordable childcare. Municipal, cooperative and parental crèches exist, able to care for infants from the age of three months at rates that are close to free through a system of pay-back from social security. From the age of three (or two, in larger cities), children can attend pre-schools (*maternelles*) for eight hours a day, for free (with the option of a means-tested after-school and holiday club, available until 6.30 pm). By contrast, the average cost for a full-time nursery place for one child in London in 2005 was £197/week, or nearly £10,000/annum (Daycare Trust 2005), which clearly influences mothers' (and fathers') decision-making and accountability around care strategies.

New mothers in the UK can expect to hear a strong 'breast is best' message from a range of governmental and non-governmental agencies (Lee 2007). In France, while the WHO recommendations are supported in theory, in practice, breastfeeding is not (yet) a public health policy issue in the same way as in the UK. So while breastfeeding rates are gradually rising, particularly among more educated sectors, the discursive emphasis on the importance of breastfeeding at the level of health policy is not as marked as in Britain, which has targeted lower income groups in particular (see Faircloth 2013 for more on this). Similarly, while in the UK, several breastfeeding support organisations exist (such as *The Association of Breastfeeding Mothers, The National Childbirth Trust* and *La Leche League International*), LLLI is the only national breastfeeding support organisation in France.[9] It therefore receives women from a more diverse range of backgrounds than in the UK. They are largely middle class (in the sense of being well-educated), but certainly not only those with an interest in attachment parenting or long-term breastfeeding, as is more typically the case in the UK.

The differing policies around employment and infant feeding were also reflected in the Parisian sample. While in the London sample only one woman said that she was working full-time, and a third were working part-time, in Paris, a third were working full-time and a quarter part-time. So, although women were on average the same in many respects – married (around 8 out of 10 in each case); similarly aged (33 years old in Paris compared with 35 years old in London) and sharing a high level of education (with the overwhelming majority having university-level qualifications) the key difference was that *many more* women with young children were working outside of the home in the Parisian sample.

In the responses, it was also clear that I had two fairly distinct sets of respondents in my Parisian sample, in a more pronounced fashion than in London. More women came along to meetings when their babies were under three months old in Paris (nine out of ten, on average) than in London (just under half), indicating an interest in breastfeeding largely within the brackets of maternity leave rather than 'long' term, as would be desirable according to 'attachment' parents. Based on my coding, just over a third of mothers answering the questionnaire fell into the 'attachment mother' definition (compared with just over half in London), with the majority of these women attended the 'Anglophone' group in Paris. (This was the original LLL group established in the city by an American woman, and while it largely catered for ex-pat mothers, there was a strong contingent of French-speaking mothers, particularly those who considered themselves at the more 'radical' end of the attachment parenting spectrum). They constituted themselves as a marginal in relation to French society at large, framing their answers to my questions with complaints about their own marginality, in more pronounced but ways familiar to those I encountered in the UK.

What was interesting, in working with attachment mothers in Paris, was the way in which they referred to the same literature as the mothers I had encountered in London – accessed online, usually in English (as many women were able to read in English, and certainly to understand documentaries, and so on). Indeed, there is a dearth of French-language texts on attachment parenting, and the only major author on the topic in French is a long-serving member of LLL France. (Even LLL's *Womanly Art of Breastfeeding* had yet to appear in France in a fully serviceable translation; it was only available in a Canadian French version that contained useless references to local sources of support. At the time of research, one of my informants was working on a new translation.)

French Parenting: Un-'Natural' Motherhood?

The American author Warner (2006) has written about her experience of motherhood in Paris (and for a more recent, similar take, see Druckerman 2012). She argues that unlike her native US (and, I suggest, the UK) motherhood was far less intensive – it was just not such a 'big deal' in France, and not something women would consider their primary source of 'identity work.' There certainly does not (yet) exist an industry surrounding parenting as there does in the UK. (Searching 'Parenting' in the Google UK site generates 85,100,000 hits; *Parentage* in Google France gets just 1,660,000).

In her article, 'Mother-Child Relationships in France', Suizzo discusses a pervasive fear in discourses around French parenting about mothers being enslaved (*esclavage*) to their children who could easily become infant kings (*l'enfant-roi*).

Rather than fostering attachment, then, separation is seen as critical. As she explains:

> [Esclavage] is the idea that mothers can become dependent on, even subordinate to, their children. This notion is quite different from the much more pervasive concern among parents in individualist cultures that children may become overly dependent on their mother. Mother-enslavement was described as a loss of personal freedom with very negative consequences for the mother. (Suizzo 2004: 317)

The worry about enslavement means French parents 'prefer more distal relations, maintaining separate beds and bedrooms for their infants, and engaging in less body contact, in part because they believe that separateness fosters independence in children ... French parents also avoid prolonged body contact, such as co-sleeping, holding, and carrying babies ... These findings point to a concern with fostering independence' (Suizzo 2004: 296). One mother in the Parisian sample, who was not an attachment mother, echoed the view that for the French there was a concern about women becoming '*mères fusionelles*' through breastfeeding:

> *Sandrine [28, 5- and 2 and-a-half-year-old sons, no longer breastfed, Paris]:* ... it is also difficult to breastfeed for longer than four to six months without being seen as a 'mère fusionelle' who is not able to separate from her baby.

Warner therefore notes that even for mothers who stay at home (and are not in paid employment), it is considered important to maintain a 'sense of self' by using childcare on a regular basis for fear of becoming too tied to one's children. Clearly, this has both informed, and is informed by, the presence of the childcare provisions discussed above:

> The general French conviction that one should live a 'balanced' life was especially true for mothers – particularly, I would say, for stay-at-home mothers, who were otherwise considered at risk of falling into excessive child-centeredness. And that, the French believed, was wrong. Obsessive. Inappropriate. Just plain weird. (Warner 2006: 10–11)

It's Natural? Feminism and (Long-Term) Breastfeeding in France

To understand why the evolutionary and ecological rationales of 'natural' motherhood (and validations of personal liberty and/or emotionally absorbing parenting) are more or less salient in London or Paris, a broader cultural perspective is required. I suggest that there is currently a more 'embedded' attitude towards the place of nature in France, in opposition to the growing fetishisation of nature as something desirable to 'get back in touch with' currently prevalent in the UK, and so in vogue in current parenting trends (Faircloth 2009). True, Rousseau counselled women to 'look to the animals' in his campaign against wet-nursing in eighteenth-century France (Badinter 1981; Hrdy 1999). But it would be fair to argue that this injunction has been rebuked over the last two centuries with a legacy of the Enlightenment which stresses human separation from nature and, in turn, other animals. As Nicole, a La Leche League leader with whom I discussed these issues put it:

Charlotte: You said that in France there is not a 'breastfeeding culture' – why?

Nicole [LLLI Leader, Paris]: I think that in England there was always, at least for the last century and a half, a culture of returning to nature, proximity with nature, with one's choices, with people – there is a conscience about children that is much more ancient. In France, there was, by contrast, a 'hygienist' culture, with a very strict order, 'puéri-culture' centres [like health-visiting centres], which set the rules: 'One must do it like this, and like that.' It's something that's very evident . . . . It really harmed breastfeeding, and it's an approach that has never really been discredited. It just didn't fit with breastfeeding, where you can't be 'controlled by the rod,' in such a rigid way.

The 1970s 'return to nature' which saw feminist movements (including LLL) blossom in the UK was not replicated in France (although Badinter (2010) suggests that the same roots were present, if not as elaborated). Indeed, 'being close to nature' as something desirable is a relatively new phenomenon in Paris, one which, I argue, is a 'culture on the make' for a privileged section of society (and it is worth re-stating here that I was working in London and Paris, which, as urban capitals, cannot be said to represent Britain and France in any straightforward way. Indeed, any nostalgia for 'nature' might be said to be a product of these very settings and middle-class contexts).

For many women, the idea of being 'a mammal', for example, was one reason mothers in France were put off breastfeeding – one (non-attachment) mother talked about it as an 'animal, uncivilised act' – unlike in the USA or the UK, where this biological, evolutionary discourse is frequently drawn upon in advocacy literature as a way of *encouraging* women to breastfeed. This ambivalence about our status as mammals was seen to be part of the country's different history of both the Enlightenment, and of feminism, as Nicole expounds:

Charlotte: There is also the fact that people think of breastfeeding as 'esclavage' . . .

Nicole [LLLI Leader, Paris]: Yes, I agree, [French] feminism was constructed outside of and *against* motherhood. The battle of feminism was: equal salaries between men and women, for abortion to defend the sexual liberty of women ... but not at all in favour of motherhood, absolutely not! Whereas in other countries, such as Scandinavia, feminism was constructed *with* motherhood. Moreover, the majority of French feminists didn't have children ... like it was a liberty not to have children. Revenge against nature, yes, that's it, a controlling of nature. To be free was to get out of that condition.

Speaking about a friend who did not breastfeed her child, Louise (a non-attachment mother) explains again that her reasoning is a product of a feminist inclination which does not encourage women to adjust to the 'rhythm' of their children, but rather, the other way round:

Charlotte: Why do you think your friend didn't want to breastfeed?

Louise [28, just weaned her 6 month old daughter, Paris]: In '68 there was a big revolution, the liberation of women and all that ... so in our parents' generation there weren't many feminists who breastfed. And even now there is an image of the modern woman: ... she goes everywhere, does everything, she works and she is not dependent on anyone and above all not to her children. When one breastfeeds, one has another rhythm, one is obliged to adapt to the rhythm of the child ...

Many women in the Parisian sample were therefore articulate about the idea that for French mothers, using either formula or expressed milk, rather than feeding directly from the breast, made sense according to these cultural norms about bodies and dependency. In a more pronounced way than in London, it was also clear that many women in the Parisian sample were concerned about preserving their 'corps erotique' (as opposed to their 'corps maternelle', as one mother put it later) as representative both of their autonomy and as part of their commitment to relationships with their partners.

Overall, for my Parisian informants, there was an association between feminism and the work of feminists such as de Beauvoir (unlike the UK responses which drew on feminist arguments *celebrating* the difference between the sexes, as Nicole explains above). Her work, *The Second Sex,* describes how female physiology renders women subservient to the requirement of the species to procreate, in ways vastly more costly than those accrued to men. Her view of breastfeeding was indeed as some sort of enslavement. As Layne and Aengst note '[s]he celebrates human society which exerts mastery over nature: "[h]uman society is an antiphysis – in a sense it is against nature; it does not passively submit to the presence of nature but rather takes over the control of nature on its own behalf" (1989: 53)' (2010: 73).

Shifting Orthodoxies

Recently, Badinter, the author and philosopher, has argued that, in the globalised context discussed above, the traditional French model of motherhood is under threat from a rising orthodoxy of 'Good Motherhood' (of the kind familiar to many British women) which champions 'natural' practices such as long-term breastfeeding, using washable nappies and cooking organic food, and impels women to take a considerable periods of time off work to look after children (2010). An article appearing in *Elle* magazine, entitled 'The end of feminism? What happens when super-woman returns to the house,' featured two of my informants, describing their feminism in a language reminiscent of 'attachment mothers' in London.[10]

Like attachment parents elsewhere, and in line with an 'intensive motherhood' orthodoxy, women practising attachment parenting in Paris speak about being emotionally absorbed and personally fulfilled through their parenting practices – which in turn form the basis of their 'identity work'. Yet, their approach to parenting, which relies heavily on a validation of nature as opposed to culture, is not, in general, endorsed in broader French culture (or by philosophers such as Badinter), which validates the Enlightenment legacy of humanism and domination of nature. They are therefore not seen to be helping a feminist cause – quite the reverse.

The question, therefore, is why these mothers value 'nature' in spite of it not being validated in wider French culture. It is true that in defining themselves against mainstream French methods of childcare, some attachment mothers considered themselves privy to better, more up-to-date information about appropriate care, and frequently cited the work of American authors such as the Searses, who they felt reflected their more cosmopolitan, globalised identities as mothers, and mavericks. The rapid growth of the online community of 'attachment mothers' also makes available a kind of cooperative support for this style of mothering that was previously linked to geographic location alone. Similarly, many women in the Anglophone group (who were not French) felt that as foreigners, they had a licence to 'be different', and used this as a platform to critique more 'traditional' French parenting practices, in part as a way of re-inscribing their own national identities.

Conclusions: The Cultural Contradictions of Going Natural

Even though full-term breastfeeding and attachment parenting might be 'natural', they require considerable diligence, attentiveness and effort on the part of mothers (arguably, as much as methods at the more 'structured' end of the childcare spectrum, despite the more liberal discourse). The strain of this effort was particularly evident at LLL groups in London, where women occasionally arrived at a meeting and promptly burst into tears. They would talk about how they were exhausted from not sleeping properly over a period of years (particularly the case if they continued to share a bed with their child, as was typical). One woman told me she had not slept for a period of more than four hours in the five years since her daughter's birth. This might also be the case with some parents who do not co-sleep or breastfeed to 'full term', but it is important to recognise the embodied maternal labour inherent to this approach (not to mention the provision of, and attitudes to, child care by the state).

The Sears now include a seventh 'tool' in their list – Balance – after seeing too many cases of what they call 'mother burnout' (Sears & Sears 2001: 112) and not, interestingly, 'parent burnout'. Following Hays (1996), it is suggested here that in the social and economic context of post-industrialised societies, following perceived natural patterns of lactation creates a 'cultural contradiction' for the women doing it. Numerous anthropologists and historians have shown how intensive caregiving carried out by biological mothers in the private sphere is a result of modern economic and political arrangements in the UK, as well as elsewhere (Ariès 1962; Engels 1972; Badinter 1981; Hrdy 1999, 2009; Maher 1992). Yet, proponents of 'natural' or 'attachment' parenting seem 'blissfully unaware' (to quote Buskens 2001: 79) of the social differences between a hunter-gatherer society and those of mothers in contemporary Britain. Hrdy (1999), for example, points out that where possible, mothers across the human and animal world may seek to extend infant and childcare to helpers (including fathers) to improve their own productivity. Yet, a gendered split in post-industrial society (with little state support in providing affordable childcare in the UK in particular) has rendered motherhood an isolated business for contemporary mothers.

Early childhood *is* a period of high emotional and physical dependency. This is not just an invention of an intensive parenting culture. As Buskens argues, 'infants do require a long period of intensive, embodied nurture. *The problem is not the fact of this requirement but rather that meeting this need has come to rest exclusively, and in isolation, on the shoulders of biological mothers.* This historically novel situation is precisely what is left unsaid and therefore unproblematised in popular accounts of "natural" parenting' (2001: 81, emphasis in original, echoing Hrdy, above). The management of this contradiction is therefore affected by socio-economic status. That almost all women interviewed in London were with a partner, white and well-educated, and that over half were not working outside the home, tells us yet again that more is at stake here than a simple exercise of choice.

Conclusion

The variety of anthropological discussion around mothering converges on flexibility and adaptation to local circumstances as the most prominent features of human infant care – whether that is Dettwyler's effort to abstract a 'cultureless' hominid blueprint or Hrdy, Konner, Hewlett *et al.*'s arguments for cooperative breeding and variability/adaptability among foragers in different environments. The broad range of flexibility and adaptation to local circumstances (*including* local cultural values) are well demonstrated by the two groups of informants here, who adapt 'nature' to work with (or against) their own contexts and cultural traditions.

Certainly, the experiences of Parisian and London women who practise attachment parenting challenge the prevailing norms in each country, but in different ways. Whereas in the UK, 'attachment' mothering (and 'natural' rationalisations thereof) might be said to be an intensification of the prevailing climate of 'intensive motherhood' (a prevailing climate for the middle classes, at least), in France, attachment mothering goes against this grain and is seen as an attack on sexual equality. Differing policies around maternity leave and so on clearly have an influence on feeding patterns – though a claim could be made here that underlying those very policies is a different cultural conception of mothering (and its relationship to nature), which accounts for why more women in the UK nurse for longer than in France. Thus, where mothers in London practising attachment parenting might be considered to have a more intensified commitment to their children than is usually endorsed, mothers in Paris who exhibit the same behaviour adopt a more 'maverick' subjectivity than their British counterparts, going against the general culture of motherhood.

The goal here has not been to show how these groups of attachment mothers in London and Paris are (or are not) correct in their use of anthropological research into parenting practices (or indeed, the validity of that anthropological research); rather, the point of drawing the comparison is to show the extent to which they construct their world view of 'natural' mothering and put it into practice in particular social, economic, and political circumstances as part of their 'identity work'. In each case, their use of the term 'natural' is congruent with the use of it in their respective cultures (of feminism, motherhood or otherwise) as popularly, if not academically, understood. The mothers in these two different contexts – whether attachment mothers or otherwise – make different uses of evolutionary and attachment theories to justify what they believe is best for their infants, in the cultural contexts in which they find themselves. They are responding to their cultural contexts and in so doing, availing themselves of some of the range of variability that characterises human mothering. From this comparative perspective, we can see that far from being 'flattened', the power of nature as it relates to moral negotiations of mothering in the UK seems to be stronger than ever, and it seems likely that the same will soon be the case in France.

Disclosure statement

No potential conflict of interest was reported by the authors.

Notes

1. This is an extended, cross-cultural comparative version of a paper which first appeared as 'Culture means nothing to me': Thoughts on nature/culture in narratives of 'full-term' breastfeeding.' Cambridge Anthropology. 2009 Vol. 28, No. 2. 63–85.
2. Buskens uses the terms 'romantic' and 'rational-efficiency', which I replace with 'liberal' and 'structured', respectively.
3. As one reviewer notes, attachment *theory* focuses on secure/insecure (anxious/avoidant) attachment based on the 'strange situation test' as a way to measure mothers' responsiveness to babies' needs. This assessment is supposed to be an indicator of the ability to form stable relationships and to independently explore the world. The table from the Sears' ABC's emphasises a host of positive personality characteristics based on maximising physical contact and closeness between mothers and babies. Quite different – but like the "natural" argument – one that is hard to dispute. Nevertheless, a justification or rationale for a set of practices the "attachment" parents prefer, and perhaps because of the multiplicity of advice and circumstances parents face, attachment parenting guidelines may provide a sense of security that they are doing the "right" thing.
4. These statistics should be read cautiously. 'Initiation' means that the baby is put to the breast once. By one week in the UK, over a third of women are not breastfeeding, and by six weeks, that figure is well over half (DH, Infant Feeding Survey 2005). These were the rates reported at the time of research in the DH and MS surveys (Ministère de la Santé 2005).
5. Research into the age of weaning in prehistoric communities actually tends to put it at between two and four years old, as opposed to six or seven (Clayton *et al.* 2006).

6. For the most part, women did not see any contradiction in being 'natural'. The only woman I met during the course of fieldwork who seemed aware of any tensions had conceived her child through IVF.
7. This was the case at the time of research; more recent (2008) measures have extended standard maternity leave to one year, with the option of splitting leave with a partner; see: http://www.direct.gov.uk/en/Parents/Moneyandwork entitlements/WorkAndFamilies/Pregnancyandmaternityrights/DG_10029285 (Accessed 02 December 2008).
8. These are the national, standardised rates of maternity leave. Some women – particularly in the London sample – had more generous packages. Women also have the option of taking unpaid leave.
9. *Save Solidarilait*, which is more strictly a campaigning organisation.
10. QUAND SUPERWOMAN RENTRE À LA MAISON http://www.elle.fr/elle/societe/les-enquetes/quand-superwoman-rentre-a-la-maison/la-fin-du-feminisme/(gid)/740943 (Accessed 23 April 2009).

References
Ariès, P. 1962. *Centuries of Childhood: A Social History of Family Life*. New York: Vintage Books.
Badinter, E. 1981 [1980]. *The Myth of Motherhood: A Historical View of the Maternal Instinct* (Roger De Garis, Trans.). London: Souvenir Press.
——. 2010. *Le Conflit: le femme et la mere*. Paris: Flammarion.
Bengson, D. 1999. *How Weaning Happens*. Schaumburg, IL: LLLI.
Bobel, C. 2002. *The Paradox of Natural Mothering*. Philadelphia, PA: Temple University Press.
Breastfeeding Manifesto Coalition. 2007. Breastfeeding Manifesto. Retrieved 3 December 2008 from http://www.breastfeedingmanifesto.org.uk/
Buskens, P. 2001. The Impossibility of 'Natural Parenting' for Modern Mothers: On Social Structure and the Formation of Habit. *Association for Research on Mothering Journal*, Spring/Summer, 3(1):75–86.
Clayton, F., J. Sealy & S. Pfeiffer 2006. Weaning Age among Foragers at Matjes River Rock Shelter, South Africa, from Stable Nitrogen and Carbon Isotope Analysis. *American Journal of Physical Anthropology*, 129(2):311–7.
Cronon, W. 1996. *Uncommon Ground: Rethinking the Human Place in Nature*. New York: W. W. Norton & Co.
Daycare Trust. 2005. *Childcare Costs Surveys*. http://www.daycaretrust.org.uk/pages/childcare-costs-surveys.html (Accessed 6 September 2012).
Department of Health. 2005a. *Infant Feeding Survey 2005*. London: Department of Health.
——. 2005b. *Maternal and Infant Nutrition*. http://www.dh.gov.uk/PolicyAndGuidance/HealthAndSocialCareTopics/MaternalAndInfantNutrition/fs/en (Accessed 29 May 2008).
Dettwyler, K. 1995. A Time to Wean: A Hominid Blueprint for the Natural Age of Weaning. In *Breastfeeding: Bio-cultural Perspectives*, edited by P. Stuart-Macadam and K. Dettwyler. pp. 167–217. New York: Aldine de Gruyter.
Druckerman, P. 2012. *Bringing up Bébé. One American Mother Discovers the Wisdom of French Parenting*. London: Penguin Books.

Engels, F. 1972 [1884]. *The Origin of the Family, Private Property and the State.* New York: Pathfinder.
Faircloth, C. 2009. 'Culture Means Nothing to Me': Thoughts on Nature/Culture in Narratives of 'full-term' Breastfeeding. *Cambridge Anthropology,* 28(2):63–85.
———. 2013. *Militant Lactivism? Attachment Parenting and Intensive Motherhood in the UK and France.* Oxford: Berghahn Books.
———. 2014. The Problem of 'Attachment': The 'Detached' Parent. In *Parenting Culture Studies,* edited by E. Lee, J. Bristow, C. Faircloth, and J. Macvarish. pp. 147–165. Basingstoke: Palgrave Macmillan.
Faircloth, C., D. Hoffman & L. Layne (eds.) 2013. *Parenting in Global Perspective: Negotiating Ideologies of Kinship, Self and Politics.* London: Routledge.
Fildes, V. 1986. *Breasts, Bottles, and Babies: A History of Infant Feeding.* Edinburgh: EUP.
Franklin, S. 1990. Review: Primate Visions: Gender, Race and Nature in the World of Modern Science by Donna Haraway. *Journal of the History of Sexuality,* 1(2):338–340.
Goffman, E. 1959. *The Presentation of Self in Everyday Life.* New York: Doubleday.
Hausman, B. 2003. *Mother's Milk: Breastfeeding Controversies in American Culture.* London: Routledge.
Hays, S. 1996. *The Cultural Contradictions of Motherhood.* New Haven, CT: Yale University Press.
Hewlett, B. & M. Lamb. 2005. *Hunter-Gatherer Childhoods: Evolutionary, Developmental and Cultural Perspectives.* New York: Transaction/Aldine.
Hrdy, S. 1999. *Mother Nature: Maternal Instincts and the Shaping of the Species.* London: Vintage.
———. 2009. *Mothers and Others the Evolutionary Origins of Mutual Understanding.* Cambridge: Harvard University Press.
Hume, D. 2000 [1739/1740]. Treatise on Human Nature. In *Treatise on Human Nature,* edited by D. Norton and M. Norton. Oxford: Oxford University Press.
Kukla, R. 2005. *Mass Hysteria, Medicine, Culture and Women's Bodies.* New York: Roman and Littlefield.
LLLI. 2008. Annual Review. Retrieved 13 April 2011 from http://www .laleche.org.uk/pdfs/AnnualReview2008(final).pdf
Layne, L. & J. Aegnst. 2010. The Need to Bleed? A Feminist Technology Assessment of Menstrual-suppressing Birth Control Pills. In *Feminist Technology,* edited by L. Layne, S. Vostral, and K. Boyer. pp. 55–89. Chicago: University of Illinois Press.
Lee, E. 2007. Health, Morality, and Infant Feeding: British Mothers' Experiences of Formula Milk Use in the Early Weeks. *Sociology of Health and Illness,* 29(7):1075–1090.
Lee, E., J. Bristow, C. Faircloth & J. Macvarish. 2014. Parenting Culture Studies. Basingstoke: Palgrave Macmillan.
MacCormack, C. & M. Strathern (eds.). 1980. *Nature, Culture and Gender.* Cambridge: Cambridge University Press.
Maher, V. 1992. The Anthropology of Breastfeeding: Natural Law or Social Construct. Oxford: Berg.
Ministère des Solidarités, de la Santé et de la Famille. 2005. Allaitement Maternel: Les Bénéfices pour la Santé de l'Enfant et de sa Mere. Les Synthèses du Programme.

Moscucci, O. 2003. Holistic Obstetrics: The Origins of "Natural Childbirth" in Britain. *Postgraduate Medical Journal*, 79:168–173.

Murphy, E. 1999. 'Breast is Best': Infant Feeding Decisions and Maternal Deviance. *Sociology of Health and Illness*, 21(2):187–208.

Palmer, G. 1993. *The Politics of Breastfeeding*. London: Pandora.

Sears, W. & M. Sears. 1993 [1982]. *The Baby Book: Everything You Need to Know About Your Baby*. Boston: Little Brown.

———. 2001. *The Attachment Parenting Book: A Commonsense Guide to Understanding and Nurturing Your Baby*. London: Little, Brown and Company.

Shostak, M. 2000. *Return to Nisa*. Cambridge, MA: Harvard University Press.

Small, M. 1998. *Our Babies, Ourselves How Biology and Culture Shape the Way We Parent*. New York: Random House.

Suizzo, M.-A. 2004. Mother-Child Relationships in France: Balancing Autonomy and Affiliation in Everyday Interactions. *Ethos*, 32:293–323.

Thurer, S. 1994. *Myths of Motherhood: How Culture Reinvents the Good Mother*. London and New York: Penguin.

Warner, J. 2006. *Perfect Madness, Motherhood in the Age of Anxiety*. London: Vermilion.

Wells, J. 2006. The role of cultural factors in human breastfeeding: Adaptive behaviour or biopower? In *Ecology, Culture, Nutrition, Health and Disease*, edited by K. Bose. Vol. 14. pp. 39–47. Delhi: Kamla-Raj Enterprises.

WHO. 2003. *Global Strategy for Infant and Young Child Feeding*. http://www.who.int/nutrition/publications/gs_infant_feeding_text_eng.pdf (Accessed 29 May 2008).

The Ethics of Patenting and Genetically Engineering the Relative Hāloa

Mascha Gugganig

ABSTRACT *This article investigates the patenting and genetic engineering of the plant taro (*Colocasia esculenta*), which Native Hawaiians consider their elder brother and ancestor Hāloa. It explores how molecular scientists at the University of Hawai'i through their research activities inadvertently disrupted this relationship and concurrently provoked a resurgence of Native Hawaiians' interest in their creation story Kumulipo and connection to their kin Hāloa. The juxtaposition of purportedly value-free scientific practices with a value-laden indigenous epistemology exposes the former's debatable characterisation as 'objective'. Scientific practices such as patenting or genetically engineering taro are discussed as hybrids that are composed of molecular scientists with real intentions; a plant as kin, ancestor and embodied god Kāne; and an indigenous people with real kinship to a non-human being. In consequence, the described case exemplifies how scientific practices are as malleable and situated as the concept of nature, while both concurrently shape each other.*

Introduction

Communication between scientists and the wider public is often defined by a lack of transparency, which as a result has often created separate spheres of knowledge production (see Haraway 1988; Shiva 1995; Nader 1996; Berkes [1999] 2008; Cruikshank 2005; Jasanoff 2005; Bamford 2007). Particularly in respect to indigenous people, a growing literature describes struggles with research institutions and governments that ignore indigenous people's intellectual property rights (LaDuke 2005; Schlais 2007; Cummings 2008; Fitting 2011). These processes have often been termed bio-piracy, bio-prospecting (Greene 2004) or biocolonialism (Whitt 1998; Howard 2001). Examples of patenting and/or genetic engineering of a plant sacred to a people point to the Manoominike wild rice of the Ojibwe (LaDuke 2005) or maize for indigenous peoples in Mexico (see Fitting 2011). Māori have also expressed concerns about the ethics of genetic engineering[1] in regard to their genealogy, *Whakapapa* (see Reynolds 2004; Roberts *et al.* 2004; Cram 2005). Bamford asserts that biotechnology has been actively confronted by indigenous people's understanding of their relationship to other life forms (2007: 153).

Taro was not genetically engineered and patented in Hawai'i until the early 2000s, and thus, in comparison to other places such as certain US states, Mexico, New Zealand and Europe, ignited a later public debate. Genetic engineering and patented taro present cases where cultural matters halted a public research institution to reflect upon its practices while they concurrently caused a surge of increased awareness of these very cultural matters. More precisely, Native Hawaiians, *Kānaka Maoli*,[2] became more interested in their cosmogenic creation story, the *Kumulipo*, and their kinship to *kalo*, taro, as elder brother and ancestor Hāloa. Stone (2010) gives a compelling review of the anthropology of genetic modification/engineering. This article extends Stone's review to impacts on indigenous peoples' cosmogenic worldview as well as their apprehension, and furthers Schlais' detailed discussion on patented taro (2007) with an anthropological analysis of genetically engineered taro in Hawai'i.

International agreements, such as the United Nations Declaration on the Rights of Indigenous Peoples (United Nations 2008), the Cartagena Protocol (United Nations 2000: 19) and regionally specific documents such as Kānaka Maoli's Paoakalani Declaration ('Īlio'ulaokalani Coalition 2003), which call for the protection and consideration of bio-resources of indigenous peoples, have often been to no avail.[3] This can result in disagreements between researchers and local populations as to what research is crucial for the latter due to diverging sets of expertise. In such scenarios, scientists often appear as 'white knights' to solve problems *they* are concerned with in ways that differ from those of a public. In Hawai'i, a public's resistance to a land-grant university's research practices exposed the underlying, diverging ethics of expertise between molecular scientists and Native Hawaiians regarding nature, as discussed in this special issue. Embedded in the context of qualitative interviews, data analysis and ethnographic fieldwork, I will discuss three main findings: (1) the resurgence of Native Hawaiians' interest in Hāloa in response to genetic engineering and patenting practices, and the hereto related redefinition of kinship; (2) an understanding of scientists' entangled practices with genetically engineered (GE) taro along Latour's scheme of hybridity (1993) and (3) taro farmers' and molecular scientists' contesting expertise, which affirm the central role of values, and thus ethics. Before that, I will give a short description of the creation story, *Kumulipo*, and the incidents between 2002 and 2008.

In the Beginning, There Was Darkness

The *Kumulipo*, 'beginning-in-deep-darkness' (Beckwith [1951] 1972), is the cosmogenic creation story of all Hawaiian gods including their descendants, the Kānaka Maoli. Wākea, the male god of light and heavens, and his sister Papahānaumoku, Papa from whom lands are born, had a daughter, Ho'ohōkūkalani, the heavenly one who made the stars, whom Wākea could not resist and who he thus impregnated (Beckwith 1940: 294; Kame'eleihiwa 1992: 24). Their first child was a stillborn that they buried at the east corner of their house. Out of it grew a taro plant, *kalo*, which they named Hāloanakalaukapalili, long trembling stalk. Later, Ho'ohōkūkalani gave birth to a human child that was named Hāloa, who became the ancestor of humans, and was taught to honour his elder brother. The chiefs, the land and taro are to feed and shelter their younger siblings, the Hawaiian people, who in turn are to care for their elder siblings, the chiefs, the land and taro (Kame'eleihiwa 1992; Yuen n.d.) (Figure 1).

This relationship was inadvertently challenged by research projects conducted by the College of Tropical Agriculture and Human Resources (CTAHR) at the University of Hawai'i (UH). CTAHR scientists Nelson *et al.* find leaf blight to be 'the most important and damaging disease of taro worldwide' (2011: 9), and also led plant pathologist Eduardo Trujillo to cross-breed the widely grown Hawaiian taro variety Maui Lehua with the leaf blight-resistant Palauan Ngeeruch variety. This cross-breeding resulted in the patents of the Pa'akala, Pa'lehua and Pauakea cultivars, which were filed in 2002 (Trujillo 2002).[4]

When taro farmer Chris Kobayashi first heard about the patented taro, she could not believe that someone would put a patent on the plant she, her father and numerous other taro farmers have grown freely for centuries.[5] Licensees were not allowed to sell the patented plant or breed stocks, and they had to pay 2% of gross sales as royalties to the university (Trujillo 2002). Besides its unfavourable consistency for making poi, a favoured starch made of steamed and pounded taro, Chris found the licence agreement counterproductive to taro farmers' common practice of sharing the *huli*, the taro stem, for vegetative reproduction. For the following four years, together with Native Hawaiian activist Walter Ritte and other Kānaka Maoli, taro farmers, as well as the Hawai-

Kalo (Taro)

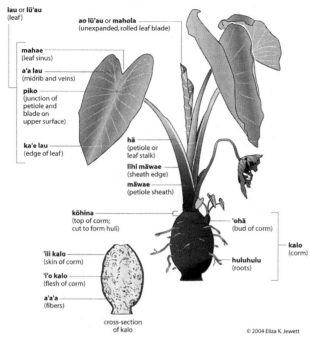

Figure 1. The terminology of kalo reflects that of the family, 'ohana, which derives from 'oha, offspring of taro. The plant's offspring are also called keiki, children. With permission from Eliza K. Jewett.

ian environment organisation KAHEA, Chris committed to raise public awareness on this issue.

Around the same time, CTAHR agronomist Susan Miyasaka together with members of the Hawaii Agriculture Research Center started preliminary work on taro in order to provide a crop-saving intervention should diseases from abroad arrive that would lead to a similar devastation as had happened to the local papaya.[6] One such potential disease is the lethal alomae–bobone virus complex to which tested Hawaiian taro varieties were all found to be susceptible.[7] The kind of potential crop-saving intervention projects that followed, however, tackled fungal pathogens. Plant pathologists at CTAHR cite oomycete and fungal diseases as most detrimental to taro, of which taro leaf blight, pocket rot, soft rot and southern blight are argued to be responsible for 25–50% of crop loss in Hawaii (He *et al.* 2013: 369).

While resistance to taro leaf blight was found in the taro germplasm, certain environmental conditions can decrease this resistance (Trujillo *et al.* 2002).

Research endeavours at CTAHR on taro subsequently involved the genetic engineering of taro via the insertion of the disease-resistant wheat oxalate oxidase gene, the rice chitinase gene and the grapevine stilbene synthase gene (Miyasaka 2006). CTAHR researchers sought to genetically engineer the Chinese taro variety Bun Long, the Hawaiian Maui Lehua and the Samoan Niue, yet only succeeded with Bun Long (Hashimoto 2005).[8] The promising results of the oxalate oxidase gene, arresting the spread of the pathogen *Phytophthora colocasiae* in taro, which causes taro leaf blight, led to further research projects where rice chitinase gene inserted into taro's germplasm showed resistance to the fungus *Sclerotium rolfsii* causing southern blight (He 2006; He *et al.* 2013: 378).

In 2003, members of the state-wide taro growers' organisation *'Onipa'a Nā Hui Kalo* became aware of the genetic engineering work and invited CTAHR scientists John Cho and Susan Miyasaka to discuss their research.[9] Miyasaka affirmed to discontinue GE taro research if taro farmers were not in favour. The farmers asserted that the issue at stake was not the kalo itself, but the poor condition of Hawai'i soils. During this meeting, and in subsequent years, Miyasaka indicated the potential introduction of the alomae–bobone virus complex that was heavily impacting taro production in Papua New Guinea (PNG) and the Solomon Islands as a justification for genetically engineering kalo. Taro growers pointed out that testing Hawaiian taro's potential disease resistance by importing viruses from abroad would be overly negligent and that farmers would be better protected by prohibiting shipments of taro from PNG and the Solomons, a point I will return to further in the article. After this meeting, however, Miyasaka and others continued GE taro research. The same year, the *Ka 'Aha Pono* – Native Hawaiian Intellectual Property Rights Conference – issued the Paoakalani Declaration, which detailed among others the protection of traditional knowledge and bio-resources through collaboration with an indigenous people and its belief system ('Īlio'ulaokalani Coalition 2003).

After it leaked out that genetic tests were done on Hawaiian taro and rumours of its possible genetic engineering spread, a public outcry followed. As taro farmers' concerns passed unheeded, in May 2005, Native Hawaiian educators, students and taro farmers held a ceremony for Hāloa at UH in order to stress the urgency of terminating research involving genetic engineering of any taro variety (Hawaii SEED n.d.; Leone 2005). The genetic engineering of Hāloa was seen as an alteration of a kin, and thus a desecration (see Ritte & Freese 2006). At this ceremony, the dean of CTAHR Andrew Hashimoto asserted that the college would refrain from any genetic engineering of Hawaiian taro varieties following their commitment to 'be sensitive to the cultural significance of taro' (Hashimoto 2005). The dean also stressed that genetic engineering of the Hawaiian taro Maui Lehua had been unsuccessful, and therefore only genetic engineering of the Chinese Bun Long variety had been pursued (Hashimoto 2005).[10]

In the meantime, in February 2006, the growing concern regarding the three patents led Chris Kobayashi, Walter Ritte and the nation-wide non-profit organisation (NPO) Center for Food Safety to write a letter to the President of UH to request abandoning the patents for their non-compliance to the United Nations' World Intellectual Property Organisation and the United States Patenting Law (Kobayashi & Ritte 2006). First, they argue, ancestry of the female parent Maui Lehua is not 'unknown' (Trujillo 2002) but had been introduced by first island settlers in the fourth to fifth century from which Hawaiians have cultivated over 300 taro varieties (Kobayashi & Ritte 2006). Furthermore, claimed properties of leaf blight resistance, tolerance to root rot and vigorous growth (Trujillo 2002) were not valid, as a month after the third patent was issued CTAHR stated that 'only preliminary observations are available on ... disease susceptibility ... and yield of the three new cultivars' (Trujillo *et al.* 2002; Kobayashi & Ritte 2006).

The letter was followed by a public protest of more than 600 taro farmers, advocates and youth who gathered at UH to oppose the patents. At this event, Ritte called the attempt at patenting Hawaiian taro the *second Māhele*, referring to the Great Māhele, or Land Division, that took place in 1848, which introduced the foreign concept of land as private ownership: 'They do not have the right to buy, sell, own and manipulate our mana,[11] ... We are Hāloa, and Hāloa is us. No one can own us' (Ing 2006: 1). In May 2006, Native Hawaiian activists chained the doors of the John A. Burns School of Medicine of UH demonstrating a *kapu*, a ban, on the university's patenting practice on *kalo* (Gima 2006). A month later, vice chancellor of research Ostrander and vice president for research Gaines of UH signed a letter that detailed the university's 'Terminal Disclaimers' for the three patented taro varieties (Ostrander 2006). Ostrander explained that '[t]he university has acted sincerely and in good faith to respect the rights of Native Hawaiians in this matter' (University of Hawai'i 2006). Opposing the idea of returning the patents, Ritte, Kobayashi and professor of Hawaiian Studies Jonathan Kamakawiwo'ole Osorio symbolically tore the patents apart (Essoyan 2006).

The university's self-imposed moratorium and Terminal Disclaimer were celebrated as a victory; yet, to this day concerns persist over the fact that the college did not withdraw from genetically engineering *all* taro varieties. In fact, many Native Hawaiians and taro farmers have noted that a ban on GE taro should involve all 'Pacific cousins', all taro varieties, as they are all related (Hawaiian Civic Club Honolulu 2008; Kobayashi, pers. conversation 2011). There are also concerns over cross-pollination of GE taro with conventionally grown taro (see Kobayashi 2008). While the risk of cross-pollination in the Hawaiian environment remains disputed, by sharing *huli*, the taro stem, the likelihood of mixing GE taro *huli* with conventional ones becomes a certainty (see Konanui 2008; Levin [2007] 2009).[12]

In 2007, State Representative Mele Carroll introduced the Taro Security Bill, which detailed a 10-year moratorium on 'developing, testing, propagating, cultivating, growing, and raising genetically engineered taro in the State' (Senate Bill 958 HD1 2007). As a Native Hawaiian, Carroll follows her spiritual belief in *kalo* as an ancestor of her people (Hamilton 2009). The bill was denied a hearing in the House of Representatives by House Speaker Calvin Say and Agriculture Committee Chairman Representative Clift Tsuji, who stated that it was 'too complicated and controversial at the time', yet that it would be revisited in 2008 (Senate Bill 958 HD2 2008; Smith & Azambuja 2008). Hundreds of protesters returned to the opening of the 2008 Legislative Session at the State Capitol to remind Say and Tsuji of their promise. Taro farmer Bryna 'Oliko Storch helped collecting 6000 signatures in support of the bill through KAHEA, accompanying thousands of testimonies in support of the measure (Senate Bill 958 HD2 2008). Three months later, in April 2008, Tsuji and Say introduced several amendments in conference, thus without public hearing, which included a reduction of the moratorium to five years, and to Hawaiian taro varieties only (Senate Bill 958 HD2 2008; Storch, personal communication, 2013). The amended bill stated that out-of-state companies that make seed crops the biggest agricultural commodity 'need assurance that they will still be able to invest and operate in Hawaii' (Senate Bill 958 HD2 2008). Further amendments included a prohibition of both the state and counties to ban the 'testing, planting, or growing ... of any genetically modified non-Hawaiian taro or other non-taro plant organism', and a ban of 'advertisement, labelling, packaging, handling, transportation, distribution, use, notification of use, certification, or registration of genetically modified plant organism' for counties (Senate Bill 958 HD2 2008). With this pre-emption clause, neither the state nor its counties would have legal power to regulate *any* genetically engineered organisms in Hawai'i.

Carroll followed Native Hawaiians' and taro farmers' urgent concern, conveyed via Konanui and Storch, and killed the poisoned bill. A few months later, the Big Island County Council passed their own bill regarding the ban of testing and propagation of GE taro and coffee (Dayton 2008), which was followed by the Maui County Council with a ban on GE taro (Tanji 2009). Ever since the failed Senate Bill 958, similar state-wide bills have been introduced, and all of them have been deferred to the next respective Legislative Session. The same year, Act 211 established the *Taro Security and Purity Task Force*, whose members comprise a minimum of 50% taro farmers who develop recommendations for taro policy and non-GMO (genetically modified organism) taro-based research (OHA 2009).[13] Then-sitting Governor Linda Lingle vetoed funding allocated by the legislature from the state budget while, concurrently, Act 71 symbolically established taro as the official State Plant of Hawai'i (OHA 2009: 12). The Office of Hawaiian Affairs stepped in to fund the Task Force.

The Resurgence of an Elder Brother and Ancestor

Environmental lawyers have referred to Native Hawaiians' efforts as a unique case in which cultural reasons were the main impetus for the termination of patents and GE of a sacred plant (Schlais 2007; Cummings 2008: 188; Kimbrell 2013). Vivid public ceremonies for Hāloa, such as pounding poi, erecting an *ahu*, altar, and dancing hula were accompanied by numerous visual artists' works that depict the human kinship to *kalo*, such as Solomon Enos' piece Hāloa (Figure 2). Ritte and Freese assert that concern among the broader Hawaiian community regarding GE was not significant until it related to Hāloa, while the movement before had been predominantly composed of '*haole* (Caucasian) environmentalists and organic growers' (2006: 12). It also expressed the reverse: a raised awareness of Hāloa.[14]

Roberts *et al.* (2004) similarly point out that in New Zealand genetic engineering has resulted in Māoris' renewed interest in their creation story, the *Whakapapa*. Humans' intervention in other species via genetic engineering is viewed as unsanctioned interference with Whakapapa, which connects the spiritual and material worlds (Roberts *et al.* 2004). Anthropologists have equally pointed to indigenous peoples' kin-related understandings of their environment (Cruikshank 2005; Turner 2005; Wyndham 2009), an approach Salmón coins kincentric ecology (2000). Native Hawaiians strive to maintain a sacred relationship to natural phenomena, which are bodily forms of gods, *kino lau*, among whom taro is a myriad body of the god of creative power, Kāne (see Handy & Handy 1978: 23). Polynesians' relations between 'natural' ancestral

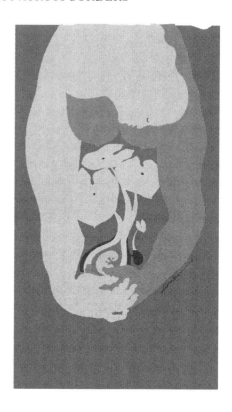

Figure 2. *Solomon Enos' Hāloa, with permission from the artist. This artwork served as cover page for the magazine* Honolulu Weekly *(2006) for an article on patented and GE taro, and seven years later for the NPO Hawaii SEED's second edition of their booklet* Facing Hawai'i's Future: Essential Information About GMOs *(Black 2013).*

phenomena and social persons are neither metaphoric nor metonymic, but synecdochic (Sahlins 1985: 81). Hence, taro is neither simply a metaphor for Hāloa or Kāne, nor merely an association, a metonym. As synecdoche, a specific part, taro refers to the whole, to Hāloa, and Kāne. In Kānaka Maoli epistemology, nature, divinity and kinship are thus interconnected, and thus differ from interbreeding. Genetic engineering crosses boundaries of species, which unduly manipulates *mana*, according to Ritte (Lo 2006). In this light, the common reference to scientists 'playing god' by genetically engineering an organism receives new meaning when in fact a physical body form of the god, Kāne, is changed.

Contested Expertise

Due to their contrasting activities and experiences, taro farmers and molecular scientists obtain different sets of expertise that offer diverging findings regarding impairments for taro's health. As mentioned earlier, CTAHR scientists understand leaf blight to be most devastating for taro, and are cautious about such pests as the alomae–bobone virus complex. The reasoning goes as follows:

> The current set of taro pests and pathogens, including some known problems that may yet arrive here from afar, is a formidable challenge to the relatively narrow genome of the traditional Hawaiian taro varieties . . . . (CTAHR 2009: 4)

The 'narrow genetic base' of Samoan taro, which resulted in the devastation of the Samoan taro industry due to its lack of resistance to leaf blight (Moorhead 2011), is often cited as an impetus for CTAHR scientists' research endeavours regarding taro leaf blight (see CTAHR 2009: 9). Taro's 'narrow genome' is explained in reference to the ancestral practice of taro cultivation through asexual propagation by planting the stem, *huli* (see Moorhead 2011: 19; Nelson *et al.* 2011). Yet over a thousand years, Hawaiian taro farmers have cultivated over 300 varieties from this gene pool by adapting them to varying microclimates, soil, cultivating practices *as well as* hybridisation (Handy & Handy 1978; TenBruggencate 2005; OHA 2009: 8; Konanui 2012).

Master taro farmer Jerry Konanui has grown tired of the 'narrow genome' argument. For him, as for many other taro farmers in Hawai'i, it distracts attention from more pertinent questions. These are addressed in the Task Force report which recommends, among other things, improved access to land and water, improvement of soil and water conditions, biosecurity measures for taro pests and diseases, and significantly more research on Hawaiian taro practices and cultivars including DNA (Deoxyribonucleic acid) mapping (OHA 2009). Within the last 200 years, cultivated wetland taro decreased from 30,000 to 500 acres, and now makes up less than 1% of all agricultural land in Hawai'i (Levin, pers. conversation 2014). The Task Force estimates that across the islands hundreds, if not thousands, of acres of ancient taro patches are covered in dense layers of invasive plants.

Flowing fresh water is also particularly important for healthy taro growth in Hawai'i's characteristic wetland fields, the *lo'i*. Yet over the last 150 years sufficient water for traditional *'auwai*, irrigation ditches, has become increasingly inaccessible due to the removal of excessive amounts of water for sugar plantations. A more recent problem is the rise in permitted house constructions amidst still active taro systems (OHA 2009: 32).

A consequence of the severely diminished stream flows has been increased water temperatures that created a favourable habitat for a pest introduced in the 1980s as a delicacy, and soon spread across *loʻi*: apple snails (Levin 2006: 59). Conservation planner and taro farmer Penny Levin finds that lack of research and ineffective policies related to the control of this pest led to taro farming being on 'the brink of disaster' (p. 11), with a 18–25% taro crop loss and an increase of 50% in labour (Levin 2006). Furthermore, apple snails do not mind taro diseases, as they would not discriminate against GE taro, which points to the uselessness of its leaf blight resistance in the presence of this pest (2009). In her study on taro farming and waterbird habitats, Nan Greer quotes a farmer stating, not with a lack of irony, that he does not have the problem of pocket rot because the apple snails eat the infested corms (Greer 2005: 99).

Another example of diverging interpretations relates to the alomae–bobone virus complex. As mentioned earlier, Miyasaka and other molecular scientists argue that this virus complex could be devastating for Hawaiʻi's taro, were it to arrive on the islands. The EU-funded *Pacific Island Taro Market Access Scoping Study* (Secretariat of the Pacific Community Land Resources Division 2011), which assesses global taro industries, remarks that in the context of the extreme cultural sensitivities surrounding GE taro in Hawaiʻi, and despite the absence of the alomae–bobone virus on the islands, the '[United States Department of Agriculture/Animal and Plant Health Inspection Service] and State of Hawaii quarantine authorities have not seen it necessary to impose devitalisation regulations on imported taro from the Pacific Islands' (pp. 29, 36). The Task Force report refers to outdated import laws that categorise taro as food rather than propagatable material while raw taro corms can still produce off-shoots under the right circumstances, and dried or frozen taro may bear diseases (OHA 2009: 50). The Task Force suggests an update on the importing policies and more incentives for local taro farmers to farm in order to limit the need for imports (2009).

CTAHR plant pathologists state that critics of their taro cultivar developments are ignorant of plant diseases, and instead locate the problem in 'restrictions imposed by government on access to land and, particularly, water resources' (CTAHR 2009: 5). Plant pathologists are experts in plant pathology, not in ecology, politics of land use, or taro farming. For instance, the ecological logic of monoculture that predisposes crops to devastation with one single disease, as was the case in Samoa and discussed in a CTAHR report (Nelson et al. 2011), does not highlight the severity of the 'narrow genome' argument.

Such a debate can also be heedless of the meagre research on already existent Hawaiian taro varieties, particularly DNA mapping, which could in fact substantiate or derail the severity of a 'narrow genome' theory. It only operates in a context of plant breeders producing disease-resistant taro varieties by using traits 'available within the *full* Colocasia genome' (CTAHR 2009: 4; emphasis added). The act of accumulating *all* genetic traits of *all* existing taro varieties, as well as traits of other species via GE, creates a hypothetical super-disease-resistant taro that makes any taro variety next to it look weak. Cross-breeding on such a global scale normalises a vocabulary of genetically 'poor' Hawaiian taro.

GE Taro, the 'Hybrid'

In a video with several CTAHR scientists, the genetic narrative of Hawaiian taro being narrow was further put in relation to early Native Hawaiians' 'weakness' to diseases from abroad. Hugh Lovell, a Native Hawaiian spokesperson hired by CTAHR as 'researcher',[15] made the following comparison:

> When you look at the ali'i [kings] of Hawai'i they basically bred within themselves to maintain the royal Hawaiian line. And because there was not too many branches on the tree, and their gene line became thin, when western diseases came they were the first to die. Same thing with taro. Taro was taken, bred back upon itself, and their gene lines gotten real thin. When disease came to hit, they're having a hard time. (2006)

The dean of CTAHR Hashimoto stated similarly that Hawaiian taro is vulnerable in the same way as early Hawaiians were susceptible to the plague (Lo 2006). Native Hawaiian scholar Lilikala Kame'eleihiwa countered that 'we didn't change the Hawaiian people. We attacked the disease' (Lo 2006). Back then no efforts were made to provide basic health care to cure Native Hawaiians, who were struck with numerous diseases from abroad (Kame'eleihiwa 1992: 202). According to Walter Ritte, Hawaiians are not arguing with the intentions of the researchers but with the way scientists at CTAHR behave like 'old-time missionaries, trying to save us from ourselves' (Honolulu Magazine 2008). Two hundred years ago missionaries wanted to 'help' Hawaiians to increase their population rates by teaching land ownership in order to make them hard working, and thus 'healthy' Christians. CTAHR scientists' GE and patenting of Hawaiian taro disquietingly parallels missionaries' efforts to socially engineer Hawaiian populations, as both groups assume that foreign elements must be drawn in to preserve the race/species.

Bruno Latour describes modern practices such as scientific research as a work of purification through the creation of human beings and non-human beings as ontologically separate zones (1993; see also Bamford 2007). An obsession with such purity allows philosophers to ignore that gods are also present 'in a hydroelectric plant on the banks of the Rhine, in subatomic particles, ... in agribusiness' (Latour 1993: 66; see also Sahlins 1996), as well as in taro. The linear passage to scientific progress in genetic engineering recreates purification in the separation of human beings from non-human entities.

Concurrently, modern practices do not merely purify human and non-human entities, but are paradoxically interdependent with the translation of the two (Latour 1993). Modern philosophers tried to manage these quasi-objects by creating hybrids of subjects and objects that are accepted as ephemeral intermediaries rather than mediators in their own right (p. 55). These apparently incompatible repertoires are 'confused' by the modernist's desire for natural entities (p. 89). In our case, molecular scientists frame and 'confuse' the final product, the 'hybrid' GE taro, as a natural entity. This is also apparent in the United States Food and Drug Administration's legal regulation of GE food as 'substantially equivalent' to conventionally grown food (United States Food and Drug Administration 1992). In this reasoning, the subject, the molecular scientist, 'disappears' in the translation process from subject to object not least to give consumers the comfort that what they eat is not different from any non-GE food. If, however, molecular scientists stress their expertise as inventors, they may return to the ontologically separate zones and define themselves as subjects separate from the object, the GE and/or patented plant. Counter to that, Schlais asserts that the image of the individual, independent genius contradicts Hawaiian traditional knowledge, which is created through intergenerational transmission (2007: 591).

Latour advocates for hybrids as *mediators of their own* rather than as mere ephemeral intermediaries, since a mediator is an original event that creates both what it translates *and* the entities between which it plays a mediating role (1993: 78). He cautions that we 'have to slow down, reorient and regulate the proliferation of monsters [hybrids] by representing their existence officially' (p. 12). In that respect, a hybrid consists of what is translated between the scientist and taro, GE taro, as well as the scientist. While a Latourian hybrid may provide a transparent and processual understanding of biotechnology and patenting life practices, the term *hybrid* remains problematic. In the context of gaining societal acceptance of a controversial technology, proponents of genetic engineering seek to deliberately blur the line between agricultural hybrid and genetic engineering methods, which has led to much confusion among taro farmers and the general public.[16] The apperception of ruptures and inconsistencies that come to full display in the demand to recognise Hāloa not as a 'belief or 'agenda' (CTAHR 2009: 6) but as kin, ancestor and god will depend on a more attentive use of terminologies, and a distinction between ontological hybrids and hybridisation as modern agricultural practice. It remains crucial to recognise genetic engineering as involving scientists with *real* intentions and plants with *real* meanings for an indigenous people and non-indigenous people.

Industrious Objectivity

In 2009, CTAHR published a report as public response to controversies over their research projects.[17] Among other things, it states that:

> Assertions of values or cultural values, which may have religious connotations, do not readily find common cause with the principles that motivate the professional activities of CTAHR faculty that are (and, constitutionally, must be) secular. (2009: 6)

In their analysis of Māori genealogy Whakapapa, Roberts *et al.* state that contrary to the idea that modern science is value free, indigenous knowledge systems are rich in narratives that are deliberately value-laden in order to offer moral guidelines for proper conduct (2004: 15). The moral guideline of the *mo'olelo*, narrative, of Wākea, sky father and genitor of Hāloa and the Hawaiian people, is for the latter to honour the former, that is, to do no harm by manipulating or owning your elder brother.[18]

Such ethics differ from a knowledge production setting where the articulation of values would compromise professionalism. This standpoint in turn becomes problematic when such knowledge production settings, academic institutions, become producers of marketable goods. CTAHR agronomist Hector Valenzuela points out that through the enactment of the Bayh-Dole Act in 1980 academic institutions were enabled to gain patenting rights to certain inventions that were partly government funded, and thus contributed to the commercialisation of ideas.[19] According to Valenzuela, this Act reflected an expansion of neo-liberal politics into public educational institutions:

> The industries at that time realised that society was gonna change from an energy-based to a biology-based economy. And this means an economy based on patents. So, everything matched perfectly, the universities were gonna move to patenting and the industry was gonna move to patenting.... So, at UH we have a big high tech or patent office that is trying to patent anything that is coming from professors.

And if you have new ideas they are willing to come and help you. So, we have some professors that decided to make some crosses and develop new varieties of taro and say: Hey! We can patent these varieties, and we can, I can become real popular, and I have patents and can start getting royalties and so on.

Valenzuela describes a prestige- and product-driven mindset that disguises the valuation of profit. In 2010 and 2011, the biotechnology corporation Monsanto granted a total of $600,000 to CTAHR for the support of education in plant science (Schrire 2010, 2011), while a member of the college's Board of Advisors is an executive of Monsanto.[20] A few years earlier, the dean of CTAHR explained the patenting of taro with the argument that Monsanto or another company could have slightly modified and patented the taro if UH would not have done it (TenBruggencate 2006). While some indigenous groups have explored patenting as a viable option to protect intellectual property rights from corporate control (see Greene 2004), Schlais elucidates that in Hawaiian epistemology ownership is problematic, for heritage consists of a bundle of relationships, and its sale would simply end them (2007: 593; see Paoakalani Declaration 2003). Andre Perez, protester against patented Hawaiian taro, makes the following comparison: 'Putting a patent on taro is like putting a copyright on Jesus, and every time you pray to him you have to pay me with bread and wine.'[21]

Hawai'i exemplifies an increasingly common global scenario where private corporations enter public education institutions via monetary means and advisors, which blurs both the ethics of the latter and their distinction from the former. Thirty years ago, Donna Haraway pointed out that a 'pallid discourse of bioethics is patently impotent to grapple with the nature of power here' (1983). These power relations are discernible in a 'growing industrial direction of education (especially higher education) by science-based multinationals (particularly in electronics and biotechnology dependent companies)' (1983). As numerous anthropologists have shown, scientific research is never free of cultural settings and values (Latour 1993; Nader 1996; Sahlins 1996; Bamford 2007). Sheila Jasanoff elaborates that the USA is a *Wissenschaftsstaat*, a state of science, which reflects the country's obsession with completely value- and politics-free 'pure science' (2005: 231). Jasanoff asserts that in the USA biotechnology was transformed from a research enterprise into a global industry, and this translates into a nation's urge to permanently be the 'first' in technological progress (2005). The majority of the public, including politicians such as Tsuji and Say, may thus see private investment such as that from Monsanto as a contribution to 'scientific progress' that translates into more revenues, a more lucrative economy for investment in Hawai'i and more jobs.

Concluding Thoughts

The incidents described here exemplify how biotechnology and patenting life practices intervene with an indigenous ontology, and how this concurrently evoked a resurrection of Kānaka Maoli genealogical connections to their elder brother Hāloa. In that sense, technologised nature, which Strathern predicted would lead to the 'flattening' of nature (1992), rather instigated a redefinition of nature as kincentric ecologies (Salmón 2000). Institutions such as universities or states have to sincerely reflect upon their positions of power in relation to indigenous communities, and thus what constitutional rights indigenous people's kinship relations have when they come into conflict with the institution's ethics – or lack thereof.

In this article, I furthermore highlight that differing expertise between two groups need a more thorough analysis of what is at stake for either of the groups. The 'narrow genome' argument needs to be put in its ecological, political, economic and sociocultural context for thorough analysis. The juxtaposition of the 'narrow genome' of Hawaiian taro with that of Native Hawaiians' furthermore reflects a disturbing similarity between molecular scientists who aim to functionalise life in nature, and outdated anthropological paradigms that aim to functionalise culture. Science is a symbolic practice (Nader 1996), as much as the human mind is a cultural mind (Geertz 1973). Missionaries attempted to socially engineer the Native Hawaiian population, while plant pathologists want to 'save' Hawaiian taro. These practices rely/relied upon the introduction of foreign elements: in one case, teaching protestant work ethics, in the other, making taro disease-resistant through the insertion of foreign genes. The logic of rendering such processes normal is disassembled via the not unproblematic notion of hybrid with its paradoxical interdependence of purification and translation: missionaries and scientists are 'pure' subjects with real intentions to 'improve' a race or nature. The end product is GE taro as natural unity, as 'substantially equivalent' to regular taro. This again parallels schemes to socially engineer, and consequently normalise, Kānaka Maoli as US-American citizens through centuries of 'foreign elements' (missionaries, plantation owners, etc.). There is a need to recognise scientists with *real* motivations and plants with *real* meanings to a people.

I have further shown that the juxtaposition of moral guidelines of Kānaka Maoli's creation story, the Kumulipo, with an academic institution's purported objectivity illustrates two things: while one group holds up its ethics by preserving accountability to values, the other group asserts to have *no* values by disguising values and profit orientation as 'scientific progress'. Biotechnology interrelated with private business (Jasanoff 2005) is not considered unethical because of its operation within a purported 'secular', 'objective' framework. This framework needs further attention if the disguise of academic capitalism and disregard of culturally differing epistemologies become its defining elements. The drive to 'invent' cannot be disassociated from corporations' investment into public research institutions as much as from a nation's belief in its progress in 'pure' science. As Stone states, anthropologists shall engage in an academy's constantly reconfigured relationships to both the state and the industry, as 'the parallels in the timelines of genetic modification and what is often called academic capitalism are striking' (2010: 384).

Native Hawaiians' continuous public reminders of the illegality of the State of Hawai'i[21] further complicate links between the value of 'pure' science and US nationalism. Members of the Native Hawaiian sovereignty movement have recently formed allies with those of an emerging food sovereignty movement. The incidence of GE and patented *kalo* triggered a somewhat lagged movement raising awareness about an evolved biotech seed industry that has made Hawai'i a centre of GE seed research and development (See DBEDT 2009: 40f). It is unlikely that anti-GMO activists instrumentalised the GE taro incident to mobilise Native Hawaiians against this technology (yet see Helm 2008), since back in 2007/2008 allies between anti-GMO activists and Native Hawaiians were rather occasional. In the recent movement, taro's symbolic power has indeed been resuscitated (Figure 2), which also reflects newly formed allies across ethnicities. A number of taro farmers comment that if it were not for the GMO taro battle, the general public in Hawai'i would not be nearly as aware of the issue as they are now. Kalo farmer Storch reflects as follows:

> In some ways the kalo became an offering to allow for raising awareness for GMO that is happening right now. It created an educational space in the heart of our community. In this way, in these modern times, the older brother Hāloa continues to protect and provide for us.

Coming generations in Hawai'i, particularly Kānaka Maoli, may further this discussion in a way that I cannot provide as *malihini*, foreigner and guest, for there is certainty that the issues raised here will continue, and thus are in need of scrutiny.

Acknowledgements

I want to thank kalo farmer Jerry Konanui, Penny Levin, Chris Kobayashi, Bryna 'Oliko Storch and anonymous kalo farmers for their helpful suggestions. Further thanks go to my supervisor at UBC John Barker, at CTAHR to Hector Valenzuela and Mehana Blaich Vaughan, the anonymous reviewer of *Ethnos*, as well as to Solomon Enos and Eliza K. Jewett for their permission to use their artworks. Last but not least, I would like to extend my thanks to Victoria Boydell and Katharine Dow for organising the panel 'Nature and Ethics' at the AAA conference in 2011, which led to this special issue.

Disclosure statement

No potential conflict of interest was reported by the author.

Notes

1. As Stone asserts (2010: 382), the terminology is as contested as the technology itself. While he suggests *genetic modification* as a neutral and shared term among opponents and proponents, fieldwork on Kaua'i has shown that on both sides critics found the term *genetic modification* misleading, as it also suggests conventional hybridisation of plants. Among critics, genetic *engineering* was generally seen as a more accurate definition (Gugganig, 2013). In this article, 'GMO' or genetically modified organisms are referred to in references and citations only.
2. If not otherwise indicated, all translations from Hawaiian to English refer to the online dictionary www.wehewehe.org. All people of Hawaiian ancestry are referred to with a capitalised 'N', Native Hawaiians, regardless of their blood quantum.
3. The USA, Canada, Australia and New Zealand have not signed the United Nations Declaration on the Rights of Indigenous Peoples (United Nations 2008). The Cartagena Protocol (2000) was not signed by the USA and Australia, and was not ratified by Canada and Argentina.
4. The License Agreement for Pa'akala shall serve as an example for the other two patents.
5. Interview with Kobayashi, 2011. Kobayashi does not distinguish between taro plants she and Native Hawaiians have grown and the patented varieties from UH. To her, as to many other taro farmers, they are all Hāloa.
6. While the ringspot virus-resistant GE 'Rainbow' papaya is referred to as a success story within the scientific community (see Voosen 2011), it remains a debated topic among environmental activists and consumers (see Bondera 2006). It is curious to note that the GE papaya, which entered the market in the 1990s, did not provoke much concern over this biotechnology.
7. The CTAHR report does not detail how many Hawaiian taro varieties were tested (2009: 20).
8. In the development of tissue culture, the Bun Long variety created most regenerative *calli* (tissue), while the Hawaiian Maui Lehua produced none (He *et al.* 2013: 372).
9. All information related to this meeting was provided by a taro grower who attended the meeting.

10. Hashimoto asserted collaboration with Sir William D. Souza of the Royal Order of Kamehameha I to form a forum/review board to discuss research raising cultural concerns 'in the Hawaiian community' (2005). Yet who speaks for an indigenous community is contested, as discussed by Greene (2004), and so, Souza's role as spokesperson for 'the Hawaiian community' is equally challenged (see Nobrega 2005).
11. Mana: divine power, authority.
12. Plant pathologists argue that in Hawai'i's environment taro rarely flowers (de la Peña 1990; Miyasaka 2006; He *et al.* 2013: 379), possibly referring to the unlikeliness of cross-pollination due to the different timing that a female flower becomes receptive and the pollen sheds (see Yamakawa 2008). Taro farmer Bryna 'Oliko Storch recalls this argument as proof of the disconnection between scientists and the practice of taro farming (Interview, 2013. All following citations refer to this interview) as taro growers not infrequently observe flowering among all Hawaiian taro varieties, as well as seed taro production in the lo'i (Konanui 2008; see also Levin [2007] 2009 for further discussion; pers conversation 2014).
13. The focus on non-GMO research requires members to not discuss or entertain GMO issues in Task Force meetings, despite numerous farmers' frustration over this fact (OHA, 2009: 27; Storch, personal communication, 2013). However, the Task Force clarified the meaning of 'taro security' and 'taro purity' in its 2009 report, stating clearly that one layer of the definition of 'taro purity' was to be non-GE.
14. I thank Mehana Vaughan for pointing this out to me.
15. It is pertinent to note that Lovell did not earn a university degree (Aha n.a.).
16. I thank Penny Levin for pointing this out (pers. conversation 2014).
17. Task Force members found this report inaccurate and insensitive, partly because it was intended for legislators as propaganda piece.
18. What defines such harm is contested, yet only few Kānaka Maoli see biotechnology as a potential tool to sustain kalo (see Lovell 2006; Helm 2008).
19. Interview with Valenzuela, 2013. All following citations refer to this interview.
20. Interview with Valenzuela, 2013.
21. Leo (2006). Andre Perez was mistakenly cited as Mario Perez.
22. See, for instance, Keanu Sai's 'Proclamation of the acting Council of Regency declaring Provisional Laws for the Kingdom' (2014).

References

Aha, Moku. n.d. *Aha Kiole Archive* [online]. http://www.ahamoku.org/index.php/aha-kiole/ (Accessed 4 July 2014).

Bamford, Sandra. 2007. *Biology Unmoored: Reflections on Kinship from Papua New Guinea and the World of Biotechnology.* Berkeley: University of California Press.

Beckwith, W. Martha. 1940. *Hawaiian Mythology.* New Haven, CT: Yale University Press.

———. [1951] 1972. *Kumulipo. A Hawaiian Creation Chant.* Honolulu: University of Hawai'i Press.

Berkes, Fikret. [1999] 2008. *Sacred Ecology.* New York: Routledge.

Black, Catherine (ed.). 2013. *Facing Hawai'i's Future. Essential Information about GMOs.* Honolulu: Hawaii SEED.

Bondera, Melanie. 2006. Papaya and Coffee. In *Facing Hawai'i's Future. Essential Information about GMOs*, edited by Ana Currie. pp. 44–46. Hilo: Hawaii SEED.

Cram, Fiona. 2005. Backgrounding Māori Views on Genetic Engineering. In *Sovereignty*, edited by Joanne Barker. pp. 51–66. Lincoln: University of Nebraska Press.

Cruikshank, Julie. 2005. *Do Glaciers Listen? Local Knowledge, Colonial Encounters & Social Imagination.* Vancouver/Toronto: UBC Press.

CTAHR. 2009. *CTAHR and Taro: Taro Research by the College of Tropical Agriculture and Human Resources.* Honolulu: University of Hawai'i at Manoa.

Cummings, H. Claire. 2008. *Uncertain Peril: Genetic Engineering and the Future of Seeds.* Boston, MA: Beacon Press.

Dayton, Kevin. 2008, November 14. Big Island Bans GMO Coffee and Taro Crops. *Honolulu Advertiser* [newspaper article]. Honolulu. http://the.honoluluadvertiser.com/article/2008/Nov/14/ln/hawaii811140334.html (Accessed 9 October 2013).

Department of Business, Economic Development & Tourism. 2009. *Benchmarking Hawaii's Emerging Industries.* State of Hawaii.

Essoyan, Susan. 2006, June 21. Activists tear up 3 UH Patents for Taro. *Star Bulletin* [newspaper article]. http://archives.starbulletin.com/2006/06/21/news/story03.html (Accessed 9 October 2013).

Fitting, Elizabeth. 2011. *The Struggle for Maize: Campesinos, Workers, and Transgenic Corn in the Mexican Countryside.* Durham, NC/London: Duke University Press.

Geertz, Clifford. 1973. *The Interpretation of Cultures.* New York: Basic Books.

Greer, F. Nan. 2005. *Agroecology, Conservation, and Land Use in Taro Farming Systems, Kaua'i, Hawaii* (unpublished Doctoral Dissertation). University of Washington, Seattle.

Gima, Craig. 2006, May 18. Native Hawaiians Temporarily Shut UH Medical School. *Star Bulletin* [newspaper article]. http://archives.starbulletin.com/2006/05/18/news/story01.html (Accessed 9 October 2013).

Greene, Shane. 2004. Indigenous People Incorporated? Culture as Politics, Culture as Property in Pharmaceutical Bioprospecting. *Current Anthropology*, 45(2):211–237.

Gugganig, Mascha. 2013. *Fieldnotes for Doctoral Dissertation.* University of British Columbia, Vancouver.

Hamilton, Chris. 2009, April 21. GMO Taro Ban Passes with Amendments. *Maui News* [newspaper article]. http://www.iatp.org/news/gmo-taro-ban-passes-with-amendments (Accessed 5 February 2014).

Handy, C. S. Edward & Elizabeth G. Handy. 1978. *Native Planters in Old Hawaii: Their Life, Lore and Environment.* Honolulu, HI: British Museum Press.

Haraway, Donna. 1983. *The Ironic Dream of a Common Language for Women in the Integrated Circuit: Science, Technology, and Socialist Feminism in the 1980s or a Socialist Feminist Manifesto for Cyborgs.* History of Consciousness Board. University of California at Santa Cruz [online]. http://www.egs.edu/faculty/donna-haraway/articles/donna-haraway-the-ironic-dream-of-a-common-language-for-women-in-the-integrated-circuit/ (Accessed 3 March 2014).

———. 1988. Situated Knowledges: The Science Question in Feminism and the Privilege of Partial Perspective. *Feminist Studies*, 14(3):575–599.

Hashimoto, Andrew. 2005. *Taro Research and Genetic Engineering of Hawaiian Taro.* College of Tropical Agriculture and Human Resources [letter]. http://www.ctahr.hawaii.edu/biotech/image/Hashimotostatement05-12-05.htm (Accessed 10 April 2015).

Hawaiian Civic Club Honolulu. 2008, March-April. *Newsletter* [online]. http://www.hcchonolulu.org/archives/newsletters/2008_03_HCCH.pdf (Accessed 4 February 2014).

Hawaii SEED. n.d. *Taro* [online article]. http://hawaiiseed.org/local-issues/taro/ (Accessed 10 October 2013).

He, Xiaoling. 2006. *Transformation and Regeneration of Taro with Two Plant Disease Resistance Genes: A Rice Chitinase and a Wheat Oxalate Oxidase Gene* (Unpublished doctoral dissertation). University of Hawaii, Honolulu.

He, Xiaoling, M. M. Maureen Fitch, J. Yun Zhu & Susan Miyasaka. 2013. Genetic Transformation of Taro. In *Biotechnology of Neglected and Underutilized Crops*, edited by Shri Mohan Jain & S. Dutta Gupta. pp. 367–383. Dordrecht/Heidelberg/New York/London: Springer.

Helm, Adolph. 2008, March 2. Commentary: Sustaining Taro in New Era. *Honolulu Advertiser* [online]. http://the.honoluluadvertiser.com/article/2008/Mar/02/op/hawaii803020334.html (Accessed 5 February 2014).

Honolulu Magazine. 2008, March. *Scrapyard: Moratorium on GMO Taro?* [article] http://www.honolulumagazine.com/Honolulu-Magazine/March-2008/Moratorium-on-GMO-Taro/ (Accessed 10 October 2013).

Howard, Stephanie. 2001. *Life, Lineage and Sustenance – Indigenous Peoples and Genetic Engineering: Threats to Food, Agriculture, and the Environment*, edited by Debra Harry & Brett L. Shelton. pp. 1–51. Wadsworth, NV: Indigenous Peoples Council on Biocolonialism.

ʻĪlioʻulaokalani Coalition. 2003. *Paoakalani Declaration*. Honolulu: Ka ʻAha Pono Native Hawaiian Intellectual Property Rights Conference.

Ing, K. Matthew. 2006, March 6. Hawaiian Groups Voice Opposition to Taro Patents. *Ka Leo o Hawaiʻi* [newspaper article]. https://scholarspace.manoa.hawaii.edu/bitstream/handle/10125/18643/060306.pdf?sequence=1 (Accessed 10 October 2013).

Jasanoff, Sheila. 2005. *Designs on Nature: Science and Democracy in Europe and the United States*. Princeton, NJ: Princeton University Press.

Kameʻeleihiwa, Lilikalā. 1992. *Native Land and Foreign Desires. Pehea Lā E Pono Ai?* Honolulu, HI: Bishop Museum Press.

Kimbrell, Andrew. 2013. Public Speech. Presented at Raise Awareness, Inspire Change. Hawaii SEED, Kauaʻi Memorial Convention Center.

Kobayashi, Chris. 2008, April 10. *Tainted GMO Taro Bill* [online article]. http://www.islandbreath.org/2008Year/01-farming/0801-15KillSB958.html (Accessed 10 April 2015).

Kobayashi, Chris & Walter Ritte. 2006. *Letter to the University of Hawaiʻi* [online]. http://hawaiiseed.org/wp-content/uploads/2012/11/Taro_protest_letter_to_UH.pdf (Accessed 11 October 2013).

Konanui, Jerry. 2008, March 12. *Testimony Regarding Kauai County Council Resolution Supporting SB 958*, pp. 18 [online]. http://www.kauaiinfo.org/Council%20Minutes.3/03_12_2008%20Regular%20Meeting.pdf (Accessed 5 February 2014).

———. 2012, August 25. *Kalo Workshop*. Regenerations International Botanical Garden. Kalihiwai, Kauaʻi: Kalihiwai Community Garden.

LaDuke, Winona. 2005. *Recovering the Sacred: The Power of Naming and Claiming*. Cambridge, MA: South End Press.

Latour, Bruno. 1993. *We Have Never Been Modern*. Cambridge, MA: Harvard University Press.

Leo, Ka. 2006, May 6. Protesting a Patent on Taro. *Ka Leo o Hawai'i* [newspaper article]. http://www.friendsoftobi.org/misc/research/tarohawaii.htm (Accessed 10 October 2013].

Leone, Diane. 2005, May 25. UH Vows to Hold off Genetic Tests with Hawaiian Taro. *Star Bulletin* [newspaper article]. http://archives.starbulletin.com/2005/05/25/news/story4.html (Accessed 4 February 2014).

Levin, Penny. 2006. *Statewide Strategic Control Plan for Apple Snail (Pomacea canaliculata) in Hawai'i*. Wailuku: The Hawai'i Land Restoration Institute.

———. [2007] 2009. *Evidence of the Flowering and Seeding of Taro* (Colocasia esculenta): *A Review of Hawaiian Literature, Manuscripts and Observations*. Wailuku, HI: White Paper.

———. 2009. Testimony in support of SB 709 [online]. http://www.capitol.hawaii.gov/session2009/testimony/SB709_SD1_TESTIMONY_WTL_02-27-09.pdf (Accessed 10 April 2015).

Lo, Catherine. 2006, April 5. Patents on Life – The Whole World in Whose Hands? *Honolulu Weekly* [newspaper article]. http://honoluluweekly.com/cover/2006/04/patents-on-life/ (Accessed 10 October 2013).

Lovell, B. Hugh. 2006, July 17. *GMO Taro – An Important Initial Discussion with Some of its Pro-advocates*. Maui Arts & Music Association [online]. http://www.youtube.com/watch?v=oD9zANrWYes (Accessed 11 January 2014).

Miyasaka, Susan. 2006, December 14. *Update on Genetic Engineering of Chinese Taro (variety Bun long) for Increased Disease Resistance*. CTAHR [online]. http://www.ctahr.hawaii.edu/biotech/image/Update-GE-Dec14-06.pdf (Accessed 3 July 2014).

Moorhead, Anne. 2011. Lesson from diversity in Samoa's taro blight. *Partners*, March–May: 18–19.

Nader, Laura. 1996. *Naked Science: Anthropological Inquiry into Boundaries, Power, and Knowledge*. London: Routledge.

Nelson, Scot, Fred Brooks & Glenn Teves. 2011. *Taro Leaf Blight in Hawai'i*. College of Tropical Agriculture and Human Resources. University of Hawai'i at Mānoa, Honolulu.

Nobrega, Mike. 2005, July 24. Biotech brouhaha. *Star Bulletin* [newspaper article]. http://archives.starbulletin.com/2005/07/24/business/story1.html (Accessed 3 March 2014).

OHA. 2009. *Taro Security and Purity Task Force 2010 Legislative Report*. Honolulu: Office of Hawaiian Affairs.

Ostrander, K. Gary. 2006, June 20. *University of Hawai'i's Terminal Disclaimers against Patent Numbers PP12,722 P2, PP12,361 P2, and PP12,342 P2* [online]. http://hawaiiseed.org/wp-content/uploads/2012/11/Taro-UH-terminal-disclaimers.pdf (Accessed 11 October 2013).

de la Peña, S. Ramon. 1990. *Development of New Taro Varieties through Breeding* [research article]. Research Extension series/Hawaii Institute of Tropical Agriculture and Human Resources. Washington, DC: Library of Congress.

Reynolds, A. F. Paul. 2004. *Nga Puni Whakapiri: Indigenous Struggle and Genetic Engineering* (Unpublished doctoral dissertation). Simon Fraser University, Vancouver.

Ritte, Walter & Bill Freese. 2006. Haloa. In *Seedling: Biodiversity, Rights and Livelihood*, edited by Brewster Kneen. pp. 11–14. Barcelona: GRAIN.

Roberts, Mere, Bradford Haami, R. Anthony Benton, Terre Satterfield, L. Melissa Finucane, Mark Henare & Manuka Henare. 2004. Whakapapa as a Māori Mental Construct: Some Implications for the Debate over Genetic Modification of Organisms. *The Contemporary Pacific*, 16(1):1–28.

Sahlins, Marshall. 1985. *Islands of History*. Chicago, IL: University of Chicago Press.

———. 1996. The Sadness of Sweetness: The Native Anthropology of Western Cosmology. *Current Anthropology*, 37(3):395–428.

Sai, Keanu. 2014. *Proclamation of the Acting Council of Regency Declaring Provisional Laws for the Kingdom*. The Hawaiian Kingdom [online], Honolulu. http://hawaiiankingdom.org/pdf/Proc_Provisional_Laws.pdf (Accessed 3 February 2015).

Salmón, Enrique. 2000. Kincentric Ecology: Indigenous Perceptions of the Human-Nature Relationship. *Ecological Applications*, 10(5):1327–1332.

Schlais, K. Gregory. 2007. The Patenting of Sacred Biological Resources, the Taro Patent Controversy in Hawai'i: A Soft Law Proposal. *University of Hawai'i Law Review*, 29:581–618.

Schrire, Margot. 2010, July 8. *Monsanto establishes scholarship at UH Mānoa*. University of Hawai'i [online article]. http://www.hawaii.edu/news/article.php?aId=3718 (Accessed 10 October 2013).

———. 2011, September 6. *Monsanto Funds Education and Research at CTAHR*. University of Hawai'i [online article]. http://www.hawaii.edu/news/article.php?aId=4645 (Accessed 10 October 2013).

Secretariat of the Pacific Community Land Resources Division. Facilitating Agricultural Commodity Trade (FACT). 2011. *Pacific Island Taro Market Access Scoping Study*. Noumea: Secretariat of the Pacific Community.

Senate Bill 958 HD1. 2007. *A Bill for an Act* [online]. The Senate. Twenty-Fourth Legislature. Honolulu: State of Hawaii.

Senate Bill 958 HD2. 2008. *A Bill for an Act* [online]. The Senate. Twenty-Fourth Legislature. Honolulu: State of Hawaii.

Shiva, Vandana. 1995. Democratizing Biology: Reinventing Biology from a Feminist, Ecological, and Third World Perspective. In *Reinventing Biology: Respect for Life and the Creation of Knowledge*, edited by Linda Birke & Ruth Hubbard. pp. 50–71. Bloomington: Indiana University Press.

Smith, Jennifer & Leo Azambuja. 2008. *GMO Rally Shakes up First Day of Hawaii Legislature* [online article]. Northwest Resistance Against Genetic Engineering. http://nwrage.org/content/gmo-rally-shakes-first-day-hawaii-legislature (Accessed 11 October 2013).

Stone, D. Glenn. 2010. The Anthropology of Genetically Modified Crops. *Annual Review of Anthropology*, 39:381–400.

Strathern, Marilyn. 1992. *After Nature: English Kinship in the late Twentieth Century*. Cambridge: Cambridge University Press.

Tanji, Melissa. 2009, October 3. Council Approves Ban on GMO Taro. *The Maui News* [newspaper article]. http://www.mauinews.com/page/content.detail/id/524344.html (Accessed 11 October 2013).

TenBruggencate. Jan. 2005, February 14. Taro Genetic Work Blasted. *Honolulu Advertiser* [newspaper article]. http://the.honoluluadvertiser.com/article/2005/Feb/14/ln/ln14p.html (Accessed 11 October 2013).

———. Jan. 2006, May 2. Many Questioning Why UH Should Own Hybrids. *Honolulu Advertiser* [newspaper article]. http://the.honoluluadvertiser.com/article/2006/May/02/ln/FP605020342.html (Accessed 11 October 2013).

Trujillo, E. Eduardo. 2002. *Patent for 'Pa'akala.'* United States Plant Patent. Honolulu: University of Hawai'i at Mānoa.

Trujillo, E. Eduardo, D. Thomas Menezes, G. Catherine Cavaletto, Robin Shimabuku & Steven K. Fukuda. 2002. *Promising New Cultivars with Resistance to Taro Leaf Blight: 'Pa'lehua', 'Pa'akala', and 'Pauakea'*. Cooperative Extension Service, College of Tropical Agriculture and Human Resources. Honolulu: University of Hawai'i at Mānoa.

Turner, J. Nancy (ed.). 2005. A Kincentric Approach to Nature. In *The Earth's Blanket: Traditional Teachings for Sustainable Living*. pp. 69–94. Vancouver: Douglas & McIntyre.

United Nations. 2000. *Cartagena Protocol on Biosafety to the Convention on Biological Diversity*. Montreal: United Nations.

———. 2008. *United Nations Declaration on the Rights of Indigenous Peoples*. New York: United Nations.

United States Food and Drug Administration. 1992. *Statement of Policy – Food Derived from New Plant Varieties* [online]. http://www.fda.gov/food/guidanceregulation/guidancedocumentsregulatoryinformation/biotechnology/ucm096095.htm (Accessed 14 February 2014).

University of Hawai'i. 2006, June 20. *UH Files Terminal Disclaimer on Taro Patents* [online article]. http://www.hawaii.edu/news/article.php?aId=1468 (Accessed 5 February 2014).

Voosen, Paul. 2011, September 21. Crop Savior Blazes Biotech Trail, but Few Scientists or Companies Are Willing to Follow. *The New York Times* [online]. http://www.nytimes.com/gwire/2011/09/21/21greenwire-crop-savior-blazes-biotech-trail-but-few-scien-88379.html?pagewanted=all (Accessed 1 February 2014).

Whitt, A. Laurie. 1998. Biocolonialism and the Commodification of Knowledge. *Science as Culture*, 7(1):33–67.

Wyndham, Felice. 2009. Spheres of Relations, Lines of Interaction: Subtle Ecologies of the Rarámuri Landscape in Northern Mexico. *Journal of Ethnobiology*, 29(2): 271–295.

Yamakawa, Roy. 2008, March 12. *Testimony Regarding Kauai County Council Resolution Supporting SB 958*, pp. 39 [online]. http://www.kauaiinfo.org/Council%20Minutes.3/03_12_2008%20Regular%20Meeting.pdf (Accessed 5 February 2014).

Yuen, Leilehua. n.d. *Taro: Hawaii's roots* [online]. Earthfoot. http://www.earthfoot.org/lit_zone/taro.htm (Accessed 11 October 2013).

Snared: Ethics and Nature in Animal Protection

Adam Reed

ABSTRACT *This paper will examine how animal protection investigators, lobbyists and campaigners in Scotland consider the relationship between nature and ethics. Specifically, it will look at the complex ways in which activists deploy the categories 'natural' and 'unnatural' in order to interpret realms of animal suffering and judge the actions of human and non-human agents in those fields. The paper is also concerned with charting the ways in which animal protection activists develop strategies for persuading various audiences of the rightness of their position; these include not only charity supporters and prospective donors, but also politicians and civil servants involved in the legislative process in the Scottish Parliament. More broadly, the paper engages with debates in the emergent fields of the anthropology of ethics and human–animal relations. It is interested in the relationship between ethics and appearance and in the distribution of agency in claims or judgements of ethical or unethical behaviour.*

'There's badness down there', Barry tells me as he lowers his binoculars and surveys the valley below us. I follow the direction of his gaze, which leads my eyes away from the exposed hills of the heather-bound moor around us, along the contours of a descending dry-stone wall and towards a small plantation of conifers. We set off, tramping once again through the long grass and trying to avoid the slope's many rabbit holes. Barry explains that he has identified a number of suspicious disturbances in the tree line: areas which he thinks deserve further investigation. After climbing the wall and jumping the fence beyond it, we reach the plantation and crouch down. With his trekking pole, Barry starts to examine the foliage breaks, gentling parting the low-lying branches and bracken in the hope of uncovering animal tracks or signs of human entry. 'Sometimes', he informs me, 'the paths can lead you to badness. Sometimes I just smell it'. And with that, he opens a gap between the fir trees and disappears into the thicket.

What Barry is looking for is snares: wire loops, about the size of a watermelon, that are widely laid by Scottish gamekeepers to trap predator species, in particular foxes, on grouse- and pheasant-shooting estates. Cheap and easy to deploy, the snare wire is simply anchored to a stationary object in the vicinity, such as a tree or fence, and designed to tighten on contact. Snaring is a legal practice in Scotland, but Barry and the small animal protection charity he works for are campaigning to ban it on the grounds that it is a cruel and indiscriminate form of predator control. He is charged by the charity to monitor and record the legal and illegal use of snares, a form of evidence gathering to assist the wider task of campaign lobbying. As Barry points out, his 'fieldwork' reveals that snares often do result in long, slow and painful animal deaths, and in the trapping of non-target species like deer and badgers. Indeed, this is the 'badness' of which he speaks and around which his investigations centre. He devotes time and energy to locating animal tracks in the woodland of shooting estates because these are gamekeepers' favoured sites for laying snares. Likewise, when Barry claims that he can 'smell badness', he means he has learnt to identify and use the scent of decomposition to find living or dead trapped animals.

For all members of this animal protection charity, snares are a glaringly human technology. They provide a simple but discrete example of the large-scale exploitation and abuse of wild animals in the Scottish countryside and of the general indifference to their ordeal. Snares and the shooting estates they are found on are taken to embody the false assumption that humans are superior and exceptional beings with the right of domination over other living creatures. In this regard, the charity's views conform to the broader critique of industrial humanity offered by the Euro-American animal rights movement. Snaring is but one more example of the cruel and prejudicial treatment of non-human animals, a form of injustice that mirrors or even exceeds human cruelty to its own species (see Song 2010: 55–56; Laidlaw 2010a: 67–68). Crucially, as the parallel suggests, animals are figured as victims, philosophically equivalent to human subjects in their relative capacity to suffer and experience pain. Like animal rights organisations and other animal protection organisations (the distinction is hazy, but in general the former are more focused on the idea of animal liberation and protest, the latter on the idea of animal welfare and petitioning), the charity sees itself as an advocate for the reduction or abolition of that unnecessary suffering. This includes the ambition of challenging the tendency to consider animals as resources, fit for human ends.

The reasoning and judgements of these charity workers, including Barry's graphic identification of badness, make clear that subjects believe they are operating in an explicitly ethical terrain. For them, the laying of snares is a breach of moral responsibility: it highlights a division between right and wrong acts, invites the attribution of blame and clarifies the virtue of their charitable work. Indeed, like other animal rights and animal protection agencies, members understand themselves to be involved in 'ethical campaigning'. Collectively and individually they are concerned with cultivating an ethical career. Such an emphasis prompts this essay's engagement with the recent 'ethical turn' in anthropology, centred round the concern to 'theorise and document the centrality of ethics for human life' (Lambek 2010: 5). In particular, I am interested in the suggestion that anthropological attention should fall not just on ethical self-fashioning (Foucault 1990; see Faubion 2011), but also upon the ethical as a dimension or modality of practice and action (Lambek 2010: 10; see Laidlaw 2010b; 2013). As Lambek points out, in common use the term 'ethical' has a double meaning – it can refer to the positive value placed on specific kinds of acts and to the general field in which criteria are laid out and judgement of action exercised (2010: 9). Charity workers deploy both usages. But, as I explore, ethics is not a sufficient ethnographic category to articulate the rightness or wrongness of an action such as snaring. At least for the animal protection charity I worked with, another mediating category is required.

As Haraway (1991: 1) once highlighted and the contributors to this issue continue to demonstrate, the construction or deployment of nature is at the heart of Euro-American debates about how one should live, 'perhaps the most central arena of hope, oppression, and contestation ... in our times'. Its definition or redefinition continues to allow subjects, among them the workers of the animal protection charity I know, to differentiate their position, animate claims to good or bad behaviour and 'refigure the kinds of persons we might be' (1991: 3). This is so despite the fact that nature at times appears 'de-traditionalised' (Franklin 2000: 190; see Strathern 1992), in danger of losing its axiomatic moral status in the face of new technologies and knowledge. Indeed, for Barry and his colleagues at the animal protection charity, ethics and nature are vitally intertwined. The latter gives form to their notion of moral authority and the former provides a language by which human relations to non-human animals can be described. The critiques provided by some of the category's closest observers (see Haraway 2003; 2008; Latour 2004), which point out the ways in which nature can deny or obscure precisely the kinds of human–animal attachments whose acknowledgement might offer an alternative moral basis for relating, may challenge that link but for the charity workers, nature continues to nuance the twists, turns and risks of their ethical lives. Furthermore, the concept is vital to ethical reasoning. This includes not only the confirmation of animal rights, but also the suggestion that their ethical awareness might exceed that argument. In all these convolutions, the essay remains firmly focused on the importance for charity workers of the orienting figure of the snare and its accompanying actions, the practice of snaring and the experience of being snared.

The (Un)natural World

For Barry, the implications of snaring are both direct and personal. Indeed, as the charity's field investigator, he is the only one who confronts snares *in situ*. These traps, he tells me, are not just human interventions in the Scottish rural environment; they are indicative of what he holds to be a completely denatured national landscape, precisely crafted for the purpose of killing. The moor and narrow valleys we tramp across, he points out, take their form from the requirements of the grouse shoot. So, estate managers plant woodland or lease out land for conifer plantations to encourage predators such as foxes to live and breed there and hence make trapping and control more efficient. They keep the heather and other foliage on the moors distinctively low through regular burnings in order to force new growth for the grouse birds to feed on and to ensure wide, clear-view spaces for the sport of shooting parties. As Barry elaborates, the more iconically wild and remote parts of Scotland also tend to be estate-run. If not designed for grouse or pheasant shooting, they operate to facilitate highly economic activities such as deer stalking or fly-fishing. If one includes the vast tracts of farmland, in Barry's eyes organised for the industrial rearing and slaughter of animals arbitrarily designated as livestock, then agrarian Scotland is not just the context for acts of human cruelty to non-human animals, it is itself part of that technology. Badness is literally everywhere. In fact Barry complains that his investigations leave him unable to enjoy the countryside. For he cannot help seeing the sinister human motivations behind the aspects that others take as innocent rural or wild scenes.

And yet nature does intrude. Snares may be a human technology but, as already noted, they tend to be laid along the paths of non-human animal tracks. Barry (and the gamekeepers who lay them) knows that snares are only effective if they are set in the right place, with an appropriate knowledge of predator behaviour. In this regard, one might speak of snaring as a practice that requires both wire loop and animal track to work together; it is only in tandem that they form a successful trap. So it is possible to identify what Barry regards as a 'natural' topographical feature at play here, and not just a vision of a hyper-cultured, denatured environment. Actually Barry automatically considers the animal tracks he discovers on shooting estates as an effect of the regular movements of predator and non-predator species over time whose actions he also identifies as a series of 'natural' behaviours. While the laying of the snare by the keeper is a cruel and 'unnatural' act, Barry assumes that the predations of the fox are within but at the same time outside the bad, interventionist environment of the estate.

Such acts of identification are conventional to all members of the animal protection charity. Concretely, the work of carefully and consistently differentiating between the natural and the unnatural animates much of what the organisation does and how its staff individually feels about the relationships between humans, their traps and non-human animals. The opposition provides the premise for campaign actions and the target for political lobbying. It defines the basis for critiques of human action as unethical and for explaining the differences between certain kinds of animal behaviour. Far more pervasive than the perhaps more studied and regularly highlighted dichotomy between nature and culture, this separation is crucial. Charity workers then still regularly deploy the concept of nature but in a way that suggests the field outside it is a purely negative space. Indeed, I want to suggest that in this rendering the realm of the denatured or unnatural carries a quite distinct trajectory from the realm of the cultural.

As Eilidh, the charity's chief executive, told me, 'natural acts are ones in which one has no choice'. They are instinctive kinds of behaviour and in the case of non-human animals vitally linked to the 'fight for survival'. So the fox hunts and kills the grouse because it needs to eat. One cannot, she states, say the same for the gamekeeper who lays his trap or the shooting parties who aim to bag a brace. Although both actions may involve the prey animal experiencing equivalent levels of pain and suffering, there is no deliberate cruelty or badness behind the former killing. Eilidh explains, 'the fox does not intend the grouse or pheasant to suffer, it just intends to survive'. Once again the distinction drawn is with the calculating, considered and hence unnatural motivations of the human actor. As Song (2010: 39) points out, the concept of 'killing for fun' is a key differentiator of human action in much animal rights discourse. Outrage at organised shoots, for instance, is often articulated through a critique of non-utilitarian slaughter. This charge is certainly picked up by the animal protection workers I knew, who also decry grouse and pheasant shoots on that basis. Although the clear instrumental purpose of snaring, in the economic management of an estate, means it does not quite fit the accusation of killing for killing's sake, it remains unnatural and wrong because it too detaches action from genuine needs.

More broadly, the identification of natural and unnatural acts is a discussion or reflection on relative culpability. As Laidlaw (2010b: 153; 2013) outlines, assignments of responsibility are central to the definition of an ethical field and the 'constitution and extension of the self'. Such attributions may include the revelation of hidden motivators, such as intention or temper (2010b: 157). They may locate accountability with the perpetrator, but equally show that 'agency has sources other than those "inside" the individual' (2010b: 152). Laidlaw highlights, for instance, the complex attributions at play in the various defences of 'involuntariness'. In this context, the natural seems to operate as a wholesale form of mitigation or to preclude the necessity of mitigation altogether, it describes an involuntary non-human actor who acts out of need and hence escapes any kind of responsibility for actions. Eilidh and the other charity workers would state that there is no malice or pleasure in the actions of the fox hunting the grouse, or at least if there is, the only determining factor is the fight for life. By contrast, the unnatural seems to draw judgement and accountability towards it. The human actor described is constitutionally wilful or an intermediary for the wilfulness and choices of another. Charity workers would hold the grouse shooter who kills for fun morally responsible for his or her actions, which are taken to reveal intention and state of mind. They may also hold the gamekeeper individually culpable for laying snares, though in this case determining agency and hence primary blame may be assigned to the keeper's employers. It may even be attributed to the whole animal–industrial complex that makes shooting and the wider exploitation of non-human animals possible.

Indeed, it is not just the fact that gamekeepers and estate managers have the choice not to snare wild creatures that makes their actions unnatural and immoral. For Eilidh it is also a question of 'scale' – as she admits, 'nature's cruel in some ways, and you will find examples of it through all animals. But again humans somehow have just blown it out of all proportion'. The fox, then, may kill and eat many birds over time, but each killing is an individual act between predator and prey in a natural environment. By contrast, the gamekeeper inflicts multiple injuries and deaths simultaneously. Not only does he lay tens or hundreds of snares across the estate, but he is also absent at the moment animals are trapped and often at the moment they are killed. As Eilidh concludes, 'I feel it is only because we are detached that we are able to do it on that elevated scale.' Snaring then is wrong partly because humans themselves have found a way to avoid the constraints of the natural order. 'I would say we are part of nature', Eilidh muses, 'but I think society is becoming more and more denatured. I think it's inevitable that we become less close to nature'. So it would seem that humans in some senses are or soon will be constitutionally unnatural.

This creates some confusion, especially when charity workers move from identifying the human abuses and exploitation of non-human animals to trying to distinguish what might make some human actions natural. 'Family units, I would say, mother and baby', one staff member responded when I asked, 'yeah that would be the most natural'. But even as she thus speculated, the woman questioned her own designation: 'You find that a lot of people don't have a natural instinct to be with their own kind, and I would say that's quite rare in the animal world, unless there is something wrong with the creature.' As self-consciously liberal secularists, the animal protection charity workers are more confident in their designation of actions or attitudes they regard as conservative or reactionary. Thus the death penalty is easily rejected on the basis that it is a state-planned, premeditated and hence 'unnatural' form of killing. And same sex partnerships are actively embraced as perfectly 'natural' relationships, on the grounds that individuals do not choose their sexual orientation. Although it is rare for them to describe non-human animal actions as unnatural, there are notable exceptions, almost always connected with what they regard as human interventions. Zoo animals display unnatural behaviour because they are placed in an unnatural environment; likewise fighting dogs or pedigree pets, whose unnatural behaviours or postures have been reared or 'inbred' in them by generations of human owners.

Of course the wider dilemma circulates around the issue of ethics itself. In imagining humans as detached from nature, charity workers may at times deploy the category as an ethical concept or talk as though the natural and the moral are conjoined categories. But they are insistent that non-human animals are not proper subjects for ethical judgement. As already suggested, the fox may act naturally in killing a grouse, but it is not acting in a moral domain, at least in a manner that means it can be held to account. Indeed, here the natural, linked to the notion of instinct and the principle of endurance, seems to actively exclude the ethical. Only human beings, the potentially unnatural and hence morally dubious animal, can choose to behave well or badly. On the face of it, this is a position that seems to reinforce the denaturing of the world that animal protectionists bemoan, to confirm the inevitable separation of humans from non-human animals.

Animal Protection Versus Environmentalism

Evidence on the Wildlife and Natural Environment (Scotland) Bill: Stage 1

Elaine Murray (Dumfries) (Lab): Okay. We move to snaring, which is probably even more contentious. We had conflicting views about the need to use snares when we visited the Langholm moor demonstration project last week. Simon Lester, the head gamekeeper, told us that in some cases there was no alternative ... Obviously, that is not the view of groups such as ... [the animal protection charity I worked with are here named]. What are the views of LINK members on snaring? Do any of your members use snaring? Do you believe that it is necessary, particularly for successful grouse shooting or game management? What are your views generally on the argument that snaring is an indiscriminate trap? ...

Lloyd Austin (Scottish Environment LINK): Rather like the previous question, this is an area that is very much dominated by animal welfare issues, which are not an area of our expertise, which is much more in conservation and population management issues. That is why, collectively, LINK has not done any work on snaring. I will ask the panel members who represent organisations that are land managers to comment.

Mike Daniels (Scottish Environment LINK): The John Muir Trust does not generally do predator control, and we certainly do not snare ... Our main reasons for not snaring are ... that we are concerned about the indiscriminate nature of bycatch, with otters, pine martens, wildcats and other species getting caught in snares. As Lloyd Austin has indicated, we do not really take a position on the welfare side, although we are obviously aware of concerns from some of our members about welfare issues in relation to snaring.

The extract above is a section of the verbatim transcript from a consultation stage hearing of the Rural Affairs & Environment Committee of the Scottish Parliament. Witnesses from 'stakeholder' organisations have been invited to respond to Committee members' questions as part of the process of scrutiny into the Wildlife and Natural Environment Bill. This is everyday business for the animal protection charity I worked with; the organisation prides itself on its reputation as a respected animal welfare lobbyist that is regularly asked by both government and parliamentary committees to submit evidence. This Bill in particular drew their interest because it was the first piece of primary legislation in many years to directly address issues of wildlife and countryside management, and to include specific clauses on the practice of snaring. However, although the charity is named in the extract above, the conversation recorded is actually between a Member of Scottish Parliament (MSP) and a number of witnesses from an umbrella group of Scottish environment or conservation bodies. I choose to quote it because I think it illustrates another dimension of the animal protection perspective, one that helps further draw out the ways in which ethics and nature and the opposition between the natural and the unnatural play out for them.

Indeed, my attendance at these parliamentary committee hearings and my close involvement with the lobbying work of the charity on snaring revealed an aspect of animal protection that, at least to me, was entirely unexpected. During fieldwork, I was struck by the realisation that the charity figured itself not just in opposition to the interests of what they would see as obvious agencies of badness or animal cruelty such as industrial farming and shooting estates, but also through a complex alliance and tension with environmentalist outlooks. In fact, at times, that latter distinction appeared more crucial to their self-definition as ethical campaigners; members of the charity would regularly point out to me the ways in which for them an animal welfare or protection position contrasted with and overrode the priorities of conservation (although at the time unknown to me, I subsequently learnt that this tension has garnered some recent commentary; see Bekoff 2013). The emphasis jars partly because, as charity workers themselves admit, the general public fails to see the division; an assumption exists that supporters of animal welfare will also be supporters of environmentalism. It further surprises because at one level both perspectives share a remarkably similar ethical stance on human action (see Laidlaw 2010a), which for the purposes of critique is usually figured as behaviour disconnected from nature and damaging to the natural order.

As the extract above highlights, this tension is also something that clearly works in reverse. When the MSP asked the umbrella group delegates for their opinions on snares, they immediately prefaced any comments with the bracketing observation that this is a substantively 'animal welfare issue' and hence outside their sphere of expertise. The second witness goes so far as to say, 'we do not really take a position on the welfare side'. To me, such responses seemed very odd, especially given the fact that the conservation groups they represented were themselves Scottish landowners and managers who had taken a deliberate decision not to lay snares on their estates. Certainly, for

Maggie, the policy director of the animal protection charity I work with, these replies and the general failure of the conservation groups to outright condemn snaring or comment on the treatment of trapped animals is a source of constant frustration. While her witness testimony to the Committee also mentioned problems identified by the conservation bodies, such as the indiscriminate nature of the trap, it was roundly focused on the submission of evidence demonstrating the manner in which snared creatures feel pain and injury. 'The cost in animal suffering is so high', Maggie told them, 'that I would like the Committee to consider what is acceptable and what we should legislate for'. Time and again, it is on this basis that she makes her appeal.

The stress is important because it highlights what for Maggie and the other charity members is the crux of the difference between animal protection and conservation. In appealing to animal suffering, she is placing primacy firmly on the life and experience of individual living creatures, their right to be treated with respect and not be subject to human acts of cruelty. This should be the starting point, Maggie invites, for any legislative action. Behind that assertion is a general assumption that the natural world is a place precisely animated by these individual lives, a fact that for charity workers provides the basis of moral equivalence between human and non-human animals. In its individuality, then, humanity can be refigured as part of nature. What we naturally share with foxes and grouse is 'sentience', 'personality' and 'feeling', an awareness of a world around us and a capacity to both negatively and positively experience and respond to it.

As several charity members emphasised, this is patently not the perspective of environmentalism. 'Well fundamentally I suppose', Maggie told me, 'the difference is that our priority is the welfare of individual animals, whereas a conservation organisation, their priority is numbers of animals and populations'. In this latter view, the natural world is a place animated by species and by particular ecosystems that need protection. Typically, focus lies on species survival, 'carrying capacity' of environments and the need to find 'balance' (see Berglund 1998). The stress placed on species inter-dependency means that individual creatures are ultimately subsumed by genus and that no species, at least in its contribution to sustaining habitat, should get left out of the environmentalist's moral concern. By contrast, the accent placed on consciousness in animal protection, as in animal rights (see Song 2010: 133; Rigby 2011: 87), allows for the proposition of abstract scales of natural comparison between individuals within and across species and between species types. It also enables their respective ranking. Plants, for instance, are typically excluded from the moral care of the charity workers I knew, and debates rage among them about the relative worth of insects and other creatures low or lacking in consciousness. Although the animal protection charity and conservation groups sometimes find bases for cooperation in lobbying work and usually collectively figure themselves against commercial interests in land management, who they depict as neither concerned with the welfare of individual animals nor with the protection of animal populations, the relationship ultimately always breaks down along that fault line (none of these actors publicly evoked 'Compassionate Conservation' or other recent attempts to resolve the tension between animal protection and environmentalism see Bekoff 2013). This does not mean that charity members do not deploy categories of population and sometimes of inter-species relations or that conservationists do not sometimes dwell on the characteristics of an individual animal, but it does mean that they both equally struggle to communicate formal ethical positions from these alternative levels or points of engagement with what they both take to be the natural world.

The contrast may be drawn out another way if we look at one recent attempt to bridge the gap between animal rights and environmentalist ethics. I am thinking of the rearticulated theory and practice of responsibility put forward by Haraway (2003; 2008). She wishes to maintain the notion that particular animals deserve regard at the level of individual and kind (genus or species), however at the same time challenge the assumption that these units of being are the proper measure of ethical concern. For her, 'mattering' always exists inside specific relationships (2008: 70). This includes connections between individual human and non-human animals and between humanity and other species. The point is not just that this focus better reflects Haraway's re-envisioning of nature as 'entangled assemblages of relatings knotted at many scales and times' (2008: 88). It is also that it offers a means to refigure the criteria and terms of ethical care. Seen from this perspective, she proposes, non-human animals are not straightforwardly victims and humans are not the only significant agents in a moral realm. Indeed, Haraway holds that an acknowledgment that what matters takes place inside tangible connections crucially allows one to consider particular human and animal actors as co-respondents (2008: 71). They may not be equal or symmetrical partners, but they are conjoined. Here, 'responsibility is a relationship crafted in intra-action through which entities, subjects and objects, come into being' (Haraway 2008: 71). It is not or cannot just be a unidirectional obligation upon the human; Haraway makes clear that key drivers of animal protection and animal rights, such as the minimisation or relief of animal suffering, are not in her schema sufficiently responsible. If one insisted on maintaining the language of rights, she observes (2003: 53), then these would not be rights that existed a priori or preformed, attached to the natural state of individual or species being, but rights that emerged over time and in specific relational contexts; for instance, the mutual rights of respect and attention that cat and human owner may establish in each other.

Although Haraway's idea of responsibility as a phenomenon of specific relations and not just of human agency in many ways serves as a critique of the animal protection position (and that of classic environmentalism), I believe that there are elements of her argument that might appeal to members of the charity. Most strikingly, the presentation of human–animal relations as particular, historically inter-subjective and mutually responsive chimes with the way many of them narrate their own relationships with specific pets or companion animals. Individuals explicitly and implicitly nod to this co-presence in their lives and regularly contrast the quality of that interaction with the more conventional relationships of pet 'ownership' that they perceive in Britain. But the sympathy for Haraway would completely break down at the point she tries to introduce other kinds of human–non-human animal interactions into the sphere of responsibility or moral concern. Notably, charity workers would outright reject the suggestion that instrumental kinds of relationship, for instance in farming or animal testing, might also be rendered as co-responsive or intra-active. The insistence that human-induced animal suffering cannot be contained within the category ethical or the realm of natural or responsible actions ultimately restricts which connections matter, a fact that also reinforces the division with environmentalism.

For members of the animal protection charity, the obvious illustration of this opposition is the act of culling. As the quoted evidence of the parliamentary committee witnesses makes clear, the outstanding 'conservation issue' around snaring is the problem of 'bycatch': the fact that these wire loops can trap non-target and endangered Scottish species such as capercaillies, pine martens or otters. Formally, then, conservationists have nothing to say about how the target species is trapped or killed. In fact, while they do not use snares on their estates, they do carry out predator control. Such culls are performed in the name of environmental rebalance or favoured species protection. Conservation groups, then, will consider and do support the killing of individual non-human animals in the interests of what they view as the bigger picture of 'population management'. This is something the animal protection charity would never endorse. In fact, they actively campaign against it. Their argument is not just that the individual life of the animal must come first, but that the whole notion of humans acting to sustain the environment is misplaced and wrong thinking. Once again, the issue falls on what is natural and whether humans have the right to interfere in the struggles between non-human animal actors.

Indeed, charity workers hold the idea that humans can manage non-human animal populations and thus keep the natural world in balance as absurd, part of the very problem they are trying to combat (and an example of why instrumental relations cannot enter the sphere of responsibility). The following view, provided by another member of the charity team, is indicative of the critique of conservation action, including culling, that they offer:

> I would argue, that the ecosystem they [i.e. environmentalists] are trying to preserve is human defined. Sadly, the wildlife in Scotland and our countryside is not natural in any way. It has been manmade, constructed. If we left it truly to nature it wouldn't look anything like it does. So when they go in there and they say they are conserving the countryside, they are preserving their version of their countryside, for their own reasons. They are not conserving one species over another because that is what nature intended, it's because that's what they would rather see.

As the quote suggests, the contrast with environmentalism almost seems to licence a view of nature and the natural as ideology. Members of the animal protection organisation are highly sceptical of any claims made to act in defence of nature; or rather, they remain fixed on the practical consequences of those claims for individual animals. This does not lead them to propose a total lack of faith, but rather to favour a libertarian solution that opposes the notion of management altogether and imagines that nature should truly be allowed to determine its own outcomes. In response to my query about when human intervention in the countryside might be acceptable, the same staff member concluded, 'If I saw it happening and it wasn't something natural then yeah I would want to do something. But if it's part of nature I would think, leave nature alone. You know who am I to intervene?' This active abstention from unnatural intervention means letting the fox kill the capercaillie or pine marten. It means notionally allowing extinctions to occur. From this perspective, there is no redemption in human action, no possibility of a deliberative reintegration with nature. Rather animal protection seems to desire a natural world in which signs of human engagement are completely removed.

Reconnection

But this is not the whole story. Although charity workers do not regard humans as redeemable or morally responsible subjects in their instrumental management or care of environment and animal populations, they do identify a basis for renewal. For them, abstentionism or active non-intervention in the natural world, which includes refraining from causing animal suffering, is a necessary though not sufficient step. Animal protection should also be about self-awakening, the discovery or recognition of natural feeling within oneself. As one would expect, this 'form of subjectivation' (Foucault 1990) inevitably connects to the way human subjects interact with their non-human animal contemporaries.

In addition to submitting evidence and witness testimony to the Rural Affairs & Environment Committee of the Scottish Parliament, the animal protection charity sought to influence the passage of the Bill in other ways. Like the lobbyists from the shooting estates and conservation bodies, Maggie devoted much time to seeking out and attending one-on-one interviews with the relevant government ministers, civil servants, MSPs and political party spokepersons on animal welfare or wildlife and countryside management issues. As well as providing scientific support for the charity's claims about the levels of suffering among trapped animals, she always showed these individuals photographic images and video footage, usually taken by the investigations officer, of creatures caught in snares. Indeed, she viewed this task as a crucial part of the work of lobbying. Maggie wanted to make sure that everyone involved in the drafting and redrafting of the Bill saw how cruel snaring could be and hence what their ethical responsibilities were. While she knew this kind of submission did not count as proper 'evidence' in the estimations of ministers, committee members or civil servants, she persisted with it because she believed the images might distress them enough to prick their consciences and change their minds. How could anyone continue to support the use of snares after seeing what they did to individual animals? This, then, was an unabashed appeal to human feeling and to what Maggie and her colleagues at the charity termed as 'empathy'.

The category is crucial to an understanding of how redemption and reintegration with nature might be conceived. For charity workers, empathy or the power to imaginatively experience the feelings of another is a key human instinctive capacity, vital to the development of an ethical life. This includes the ability to feel non-human animal joy and suffering. As one staff member told me, 'when every child is born they have a connection with animals'.

The tragedy is that as the child grows into society he or she is taught to lose that connection and instead develop sets of unnatural reactions that result in detachment, animal cruelty and exploitation. Drawing on literature in child protection (see Myers 2013), an area at least one member of staff had previously worked in, the charity claims that the withdrawal of this empathy and sympathetic relationship to animals also explains cruelty and abuse between humans. There is a strong sense, then, of an ethical sensibility lost but still latent within us that if recovered might radically reconstitute not just human–animal relations, but also relations between people. In showing the images of trapped creatures Maggie is therefore simply aiming to revive a basic humanity, to enable subjects to reconnect.

Such a strategy was based in sound experience from another domain of the charity's work, the field of public campaigning. Like many animal rights organisations (see Song 2010), it had found that the display or publication of images of animal cruelty was a highly successful way of engaging supporters in particular issues and persuading them to 'take action'. In the case of the 'Ban Snaring' campaign, photographs and footage of foxes or badgers caught and struggling in snares or of the sometimes horrific injuries that killed them were crucial components that led individuals to sign petitions, fill out the template and send a letter to local MSPs or donate money. The images were regularly used in public talks and debates, school visits and on election hustings. Maggie also displayed them at stall presentations during the annual conferences of the main political parties, using the images to target ordinary delegates as much as the elected representatives. Indeed, at conference fringe meetings organised to discuss snaring, she regularly chose to illustrate her talk with a slideshow of animal suffering. Video footage of injured, distressed or dead trapped creatures often played on a continuous loop throughout the Q&A sessions that followed, provoking supportive but notably passionate, angry or tearful contributions from the floor. Before leaving such events, many of those present committed themselves to campaign for a ban on snaring, to lobby their parliamentary and local authority representatives and other branch party members.

To Maggie, the response of the delegates at these fringe meeting was not unexpected. There seems an assumption that snares, or at least images of animals trapped in snares, have the power to radically impact an audience and motivate grassroots dissent. Like other members of the animal protection charity, she views the public reaction as entirely 'natural'. Indeed, she believes that these images work precisely because they draw out 'innate connections'. Snares, then, may act as instruments of predator control and animal suffering, but once reproduced and displayed in campaign literature and media, they can also become a kind of empathy-making machine, eliciting or trapping human feeling for the snared creatures.

This idea of an ethics that needs to be aggressively sparked or reignited through mediated encounters with suffering is essential. It informs not just the way Maggie and other charity workers figure the power of images to instil empathy (or snare an audience), but also their broader sense of how human subjects come to ethical awareness. Individuals, for instance, consistently told me that they first developed a sense of their own moral obligations to non-human animals through encounters or personal experiences with particular creatures. Accounts of these relationships, often begun in childhood, remain crucial for them, to the extent that they tend to subsume the formal giving of reasons or moral logic such as the language of rights. In fact, it was this original feeling or experience of empathy with an animal, usually a household pet, that usually led them to later seek out and discover the literature on animal cruelty and animal rights and to involve themselves in campaigning. The chronology is important because it explains charity members' attitude to abstract moral reasoning and deployment of scientific evidence. While staff regularly make use of both – the latter in part because it is the required form of legislative lobbying – and regard them as valuable, they are ultimately treated as secondary means of persuasion and after-the-fact confirmatory methods for reaching an ethical stance. For charity workers claim that they already instinctively know that animals are sentient, just as they already know through their own encounters that individual non-human creatures can possess distinctive personalities. As a natural or innate kind of human knowing, such a basis for morality is, they hold, vitally democratic. The animal protection charity believes that empathy can be potentially reawakened in everyone, humanity retrospectively revealed as natural after all.

Conclusion

To me, the notion of the charity workers seems to chime with an idea of ethics as 'disruptive event' (Smith 2011: 33–34; see Levinas 2003), an occurrence that dramatically interrupts commonplace and self-oriented interests. As Smith highlights, such a happening may be understood as motivated and delivered through direct or mediated experience of a singularity that is not one's own and which thus forces recognition of responsibility; although the encounter is with an individual being, it seems to call forth a wider concern, for like beings in equivalent situations (such as all creatures trapped in snares).

Indeed, Smith postulates that this kind of 'fellow feeling' (2011: 27), invoked and re-invoked by attention and response to the appearance of another, is perhaps a more accurate reflection of how ethical obligation and evaluation grows.

This may be so, but that attention to the fellow feeling sparked by appearances, including images of snared creatures, does not however lead charity workers to consciously challenge or redefine their vision of nature. Unlike Smith (2011: 38), they do not suggest that one might begin to consider it as a dynamic process of manifestation, 'the continual unfolding of existence into the phenomenal world of appearances'. Equally, they do not seek to critique the treatment of nature as a 'premature assemblage' (Latour 2004) or to re-narrate the human within the natural through a focus on relatings (Haraway 2008). For them, nature is still self-evidently nature, and remains valued as a whole ethically. This is so despite the fact that they offer stringent critiques of the ways others construct nature; they are quite prepared, for instance, to reveal its ideological foundation in the hands of conservationists. Although environments may be denatured and our treatment of animals dominated by instrumental and unnatural acts (typified by the laying of snares), faith exists that natural feeling persists and, if human action allows, can even flourish.

Acknowledgments

I would like to thank all the members of the animal protection charity that I work with, including past and current staff. My thanks to Katie Dow and Victoria Boydell for inviting me to contribute to this special volume. I am also grateful for the comments and feedback of the reviewers, and those provided informally by Eeva Berglund, Matei Candea, Robin Irvine, Annelise Riles, Shari Sabeti and Tom Yarrow. Versions of this paper were given in anthropology department seminars at Durham, Maynooth and St Andrews, and I thank those audiences too.

Disclosure statement

No potential conflict of interest was reported by the author.

References

Bekoff, Marc (ed.). 2013. *Ignoring Nature No More: The Case for Compassionate Conservation*. Chicago, IL: University of Chicago Press.

Berglund, Eeva. 1998. *Knowing Nature, Knowing Science: Ethnology of Environmental Activism*. Cambridge: The White Horse Press.

Faubion, James. 2011. *An Anthropology of Ethics*. Cambridge: Cambridge University Press.

Foucault, Michel. 1990. *The Use of Pleasure*. (Robert Hurley, Trans.). New York, NY: Vintage Books.

Franklin, Sarah. 2000. Life Itself: Global Nature and the Genetic Imaginary. In *Global Nature, Global Culture*, edited by Sarah Franklin, Celia Lury and Jackie Stacey. pp. 188–227. London: Sage.

Haraway, Donna J. 1991. *Simians, Cyborgs, and Women: the reinvention of Nature*. New York, NY: Routledge.
——. 2003. *The Companion Species Manifesto: Dogs, People, and Significant Otherness*. Chicago, IL: Prickly Paradigm Press.
——. 2008. *When Species Meet*. Minneapolis: University of Minnesota Press.
Laidlaw, James. 2010a. Ethical Traditions in Question: Diaspora Jainism and the Environmental and Animal Liberation Movements. In *Ethical Life in South Asia*, edited by Anand Pandian and Daud Ali. pp. 61–80. Bloomington: Indiana University Press.
——. 2010b. Agency and Responsibility: Perhaps You Can Have Too Much of a Good Thing. In *Ordinary Ethics: Anthropology, Language and Action*, edited by Michael Lambek. pp. 143–164. New York, NY: Fordham University Press.
——. 2013. *The Subject of Virtue: An Anthropology of Ethics and Freedom (New Departures in Anthropology)*. Cambridge: Cambridge University Press.
Lambek, Michael. 2010. Introduction. In *Ordinary Ethics: Anthropology, Language and Action*, edited by Michael Lambek. pp. 1–38. New York, NY: Fordham University Press.
Latour, Bruno. 2004. *Politics of Nature: How to Bring the Sciences into Democracy*. Cambridge, MA: Harvard University Press.
Levinas, Emmanuel. 2003. *Humanism of the Other*. Urbana: University of Illinois Press.
Myers Jr. Olin Eugene. 2013. Children, Animals, and Social Neuroscience: Empathy, Conservation Education, and Activism. In *Ignoring Nature No More: the Case for Compassionate Conservation*, edited by Marc Bekoff. pp. 271–286. Chicago, IL: University of Chicago Press.
Rigby, Kate. 2011. Getting a Taste for the Bogong Moth. *Australian Humanities Review*, 50:77–94.
Smith, Mick. 2011. Dis(appearance): Earth, Ethics and Apparently (In)significant Others. *Australian Humanities Review*, 50:23–44.
Song, Hoon. 2010. *Pigeon Trouble: Bestiary biopolitics in a deindustrialised America*. Philadelphia: University of Pennsylvania Press.
Strathern, Marilyn. 1992. *After Nature: English Kinship in the Late Twentieth Century*. Cambridge: Cambridge University Press.

'A Nine-Month Head-Start':
The Maternal Bond and Surrogacy

Katharine Dow

ABSTRACT *This article analyses how interviewees drew on the 'natural' concept of the maternal bond to make nuanced and contingent claims about motherhood and the ethics of surrogacy. Based on ethnographic fieldwork in Scotland with people who do not have personal experience of surrogacy, it describes how they used this 'natural' concept to make claims about the ethics of surrogacy and compares these claims with their personal experiences of maternal bonding. Interviewees expected that because of the experience of pregnancy, mothers have a 'nine-month head-start' in bonding with their children. While this valorises it, it also reproduces normative expectations about the nature and ethic of motherhood.*

'A Nine-Month Head-Start'

One afternoon towards the end of my fieldwork in northeast Scotland, I was sitting talking with Erin. I had spent quite some time with her and her family over the previous 18 months and had got to know her well. Now, she had agreed to let me record an interview with her about her thoughts on surrogacy. While her daughter was at nursery school, we talked for a couple of hours – about surrogacy, but also about Erin's personal experience of motherhood, which had come somewhat unexpectedly as she had been told that she was unlikely to conceive a child after sustaining serious abdominal injuries in a car accident as a teenager.

Erin, who had always wanted to be a mother, conceived her daughter on honeymoon and her pregnancy was a wonderful surprise. She described feeling a 'special bond' starting to form with her unborn daughter from the moment she had a positive pregnancy test:

> [F]or me, part of this special bond was, all the way through the pregnancy, my intestines were being kicked to bits, I was the one on the loo twenty times a day, but it was actually something that [my husband] could only participate in to a point. You know, I could say, 'ooh look, come and feel this baby kicking', but you already have a psychological and emotional bond ... if you like, I got a nine-month head-start on the bloke concerned and I think you can't compete with that and I think that makes mummies that carry their own children special in their own right.

By emphasising her intimate, physical connection to her daughter through her phrase 'a nine-month head-start', Erin located her bond with her in both a different time and place, which her husband could not access because of his different physiological relationship to her. In this article, I will analyse the effects of this idea that mothers experience a unique and special bond formed during pregnancy with their children. Specifically, I will describe the importance of ideas of nature and naturalness in motherhood by comparing participants' own experiences and observations of maternal bonding[1] with their ideas about maternal bonding in surrogacy.

This article is based on 20 months' ethnographic research in northeast Scotland between 2006 and 2007. I investigated what surrogacy, which is a practice that has provoked intense and sustained public and ethical debate in the UK and elsewhere, means to people like Erin who are not personally involved in it and how their ethical claims about surrogacy relate to their more everyday concerns and values. The participants are white, middle-class and university-educated, work in the public or voluntary sector and they are largely left of centre in their politics.

The participants in this project talked about surrogacy as an ethical issue, discussing the right and wrong ways in which it should be handled, typically using the language of nature and naturalness and focusing on the emotional ramifications it might have for those involved. They assumed that the motivations of intended parents in surrogacy arrangements were self-evident: they 'naturally' wanted to have children 'of their own' (i.e. to whom at least one of them was genetically related). In our conversations they focused much more on surrogate mothers, who seemed to be the most problematic parties in these agreements, as they challenge fundamental precepts about both the 'given' and 'made' – that is, those things that seem automatic and those which are built up gradually – aspects of motherhood – and, by extension, femininity and kinship.

The maternal bond appeared to the participants in my research to be a natural phenomenon – and therefore stable, universal and automatic. But, in our discussions about surrogate mothers bonding or not bonding with the children they carry showed they formulated and expressed it in different, and sometimes contradictory, ways. Like nature, which is itself a highly polysemous concept, they appealed to the concept of the maternal bond as if it were stable, while deploying it creatively to make particular and partisan claims. It is this multifaceted quality, as well as its association with the natural, that gives the maternal bond its rhetorical and moral purchase. Because a woman who has gestated and given birth to a child is supposed to give that child up to another person's care at birth, surrogacy destabilises the popular status of the maternal bond as a natural phenomenon arising inevitably out of embodied experience; it is this aspect of the ethical dilemmas provoked by surrogacy that I will concentrate on here.

I collected data through participant observation and interviews. As a participant observer, I was involved in the lives of around 60 people and carried out semi-formal interviews with 30 women and men aged from their twenties to their sixties. I used this methodology to formulate a contextualised analysis of how people make ethical judgements, relating my observations of their everyday practice to the claims they made about surrogacy in interviews, tracing the connections between their moral values and ethical decisions in claims and in practice.

This article takes one particular aspect of what people in northeast Scotland said to me about surrogacy, which is the problem of surrogate mothers (not) forming a bond with the children they carry for the intended parents. Rather than treating their thoughts about maternal bonding and surrogacy in isolation, it also relates their observations and experiences of maternal bonding from their own lives in order to both provide context to their judgements on surrogacy and to show the contingent and strategic ways in which they drew upon the idea of the 'natural' phenomenon of the maternal bond. This focus on maternal bonding emerged from the interviewees' responses.

The Nature of Motherhood

Nature and ideas of naturalness are key to ideas about motherhood and, in particular, *good* mothering. While there is no shortage of work on motherhood and variant forms of mothering within the social sciences, the profundity of its significance for how we think about ourselves, and our relationships with others, can sometimes get lost in the cracks between academic disciplines and in our own cultural assumptions about the naturalness of this primary relationship. Motherhood is thought, in the UK, to be driven by 'natural' forces, from the nebulous concept of maternal instinct to the influences of hormones such as oxytocin on the body. Along with this, there has been an increasing shift towards a 'child-centred' intensive parenting philosophy which prioritises the needs of children over their parents, yet which also reproduces an expectation that mothers will be the primary caregivers and which demands high investments of time, money and emotional labour (see Hays 1996; Faircloth *et al.* 2013; Lee *et al.* 2014).

Some time ago, Drummond (1978) examined earlier forms of 'mother surrogation', including the work of domestic nannies in raising and rearing middle- and upper-class English children.[2] He showed that, not only is there variation in motherhood between different cultures, but that even within English society, the mother concept is, and has historically been, 'internally inconsistent' (1978: 40). Traditional practices like nannying, fosterage and wet-nursing split maternal roles between different women and brought financial reward into maternal labour; historically, 'blood ties' have been emphasised or de-emphasised for particular purposes and different aspects of motherhood have been more or less defined by physical or emotional nurturance.[3] Drummond's analysis reminds us that there is a long history of maternal labour being split between different women, but also that perceptions of such practices depend on contemporary discourses and ethics. Wet-nursing became popular in the context of a particular classed division of labour but it was also possible because the idea of maternal bonding had less salience at the time.

The historical contingency of maternal bonding is highly relevant to techniques of assisted conception including in particular surrogacy, since such 'natural' phenomena may need to be carefully managed in infertility clinics to avoid multiple and competing claims to parenthood. Various anthropologists have shown that those personally involved in surrogacy arrangements use concepts like nature and maternity strategically, in order to preserve the claims of intended parents and to place surrogacy within a more socially acceptable frame (see Ragoné 1994; Thompson 2001; Teman 2010). In particular, Thompson has described the 'strategic naturalizing' of patients in infertility clinics in America – she describes the clinic as:

> a site where certain bases of kin differentiation are foregrounded and recrafted while others are minimalized to make the couples who seek and pay for infertility treatment – the intended parents – come out through legitimate and intact chains of descent as the real parents. (2005: 145)

As she says in relation to the surrogacy cases she encountered in the field, there seems to be an 'absence of a unique biological ground for answering the question, "who is the mother?"' (2005: 177), yet through creative and strategic mobilisation of the possible answers to this question, patients and clinicians were usually able to create compelling arguments for each particular case, which drew on both biological and cultural factors to preserve procreative intent, kinship claims and gender identity.

The continued coverage of surrogacy arrangements in the media and the ongoing debate over surrogacy in feminist philosophy (see Corea 1985; Stanworth 1987; Zipper & Sevenhuijsen 1987; Anderson 1990 for some early and influential examples and Cooper & Waldby 2014 for a more recent approach) show how surrogacy provokes intense cultural, ethical and political anxieties (see Strathern 1992a; 1992b; 2003; Edwards *et al.* 1993; Cook *et al.* 2003). This continues to this day, though the focus of research most recently has turned to the burgeoning transnational surrogacy industry.

There is empirical evidence that surrogacy can be distressing and exploitative for those involved and as such it has received attention from bioethicists, feminist scholars and from the point of view of reproductive justice (see, for example, Pande 2009; 2010). But, on the level of public debate and ethical judgements in the UK which is my focus here, the reason why it is so contentious is because it upturns taken-for-granted beliefs about the nature of motherhood and challenges normative ideas about kinship and femininity. Where once maternity seemed certain because a child's mother could only be the woman who had given birth to her, with surrogacy and egg donation, opportunities to have more than one 'biological' mother are opened up (Ragoné 1994; Strathern 2003; Konrad 2005), though, as discussed above, practices like wet-nursing show that motherhood has never been entirely singular. However, as Franklin (2013) has recently shown, despite the challenges that assisted reproductive technologies present to deeply held views about kinship, parenthood and gender, in practice they often have the effect of reinforcing heteronormative models of family formation and conjugal relationships.

Surrogacy, like other assisted reproductive technologies, has typically been studied by social scientists in infertility clinics and surrogacy agencies, and from the point of view of those using this reproductive technology (see Ragoné 1994; Roberts 1998; Teman 2003; 2010; Thompson 2005). In the UK, surrogacy has not been quite as normalised as in vitro fertilisation (IVF) and it continues to have an important place in the public imagination as an ethical 'problem' that crosses, or at least stretches, ethical boundaries. Viewed from the outside, it seems to signify changing family constitutions, scientific and technological progress, the ability of people to overcome what once seemed natural or god-given conditions and the possibility that women's reproductive capacities might become subject to market forces. It is this gap between public and policy discussions of surrogacy on the one hand and personal experiences that my research addresses, by asking what people who do not have a personal stake in surrogacy, but who are aware of the practice through media and public debate, think about its ethics.

In a time of assisted reproductive technologies, public concern about parenting practices and more general fears about the future of the natural world, motherhood has become a focus for a range of wider anxieties about demographic change, shifting gender roles and the health of future generations (see also Dow 2013). This article analyses how interviewees drew on the 'natural' concept of the maternal bond to make nuanced claims about motherhood and the ethics of surrogacy. Based on the empirical data presented, it makes two arguments: that the 'nine-month head-start' of the maternal bond reproduces the normative expectation that mothers are predisposed towards being children's primary caregivers and that 'natural' concepts like the maternal bond are used contingently and strategically in ethical judgements about reproduction and parenting.

A Vital Difference

The purchase that the relationship between mother and child has had on psychological theory suggests the deep significance of this relationship to how we conceptualise identity, sexuality, kinship and gender, among other things. From Freud to Bowlby, psychoanalysts and psychologists have assumed that unhealthy attachments between mother and child create higher risks of mental, and even physical, ill health for the child later in life. Attachment theory may have lost some of its former authority for psychologists, yet ideas about mother-child bonding are inherent in popular parenting culture (see Eyer 1992; Wall 2001; Suizzo 2004; Davis 2008; Faircloth 2013; Lee *et al.* 2014) and current social and public policy is underlain by an assumption that a positive early experience of mother-child bonding is vital to giving children the right start in life (Lee *et al.* 2014). Ideas about maternal bonding reflect a sense that relationships need nurturing, that responsibility needs fostering and that nature can help guide good mothering.

Before discussing the importance of maternal bonding to surrogacy for the people I interviewed in northeast Scotland, in this section I will outline their sense of the importance of maternal bonding more generally by describing their own experiences and observations of maternal bonding. For participants in my research, whether or not they have children, the maternal bond is a psychological and emotional attachment that arises naturally and inevitably out of the embodied experience of pregnancy. Like Erin, they all thought of the maternal bond as compelling mothers towards particular kinds of behaviours and relationships, including specifically a sense of ultimate responsibility for the dependent child.

Nina was in her early twenties and worked for an animal conservation charity. She comes from the Highlands and her partner is in the Royal Air Force. She told me that she planned to have children in the future and that if she had trouble conceiving 'naturally' she would prefer to use assisted conception to adopting, because she was concerned that it would not be 'enough' for her:

> Yeah, it's just carrying on the family line, I guess, and I don't know if you'd ever have quite the same bond with a child that you'd adopted, even from a baby, with a child that had actually come from you and you'd had inside you for nine months. I think that's – it might be different for men and women – because, you know carrying a child for nine months, you're bonding with it for all that time. Whereas, adoption, you don't really get the whole thing, you just get the baby, you don't get the whole experience that goes with it. I think just being pregnant, before you even get the child, is a big part of it, and something that every woman maybe wants to experience.

For Nina, being pregnant is an important part of being a woman, but carrying and giving birth to a child is also about safeguarding the formation of a bond between mother and child.

I had many conversations with mothers who recounted stories of difficult births and admitted the pressures, as well as the rewards, of parenthood. Many of these comments suggested that bonds between mothers and children need to be worked on, implying that, while maternal bonding may be something that begins 'naturally', its full development is not always inevitable or automatic, but must be nurtured, though the specific embodied experience of pregnancy also implies that women are predisposed towards such nurturance. This is consistent with Davis' (2008) research among mothers of different ages in Scotland. Davis found that bonding with their children was something that mothers expected to happen, but that in reality it entailed work and time. For the mothers she interviewed 'maternal instinct' was on the one hand a complex of emotions, especially protectiveness and deep love, which seemed to arise naturally, while on the other hand it was the intimate and personal knowledge of one's child that comes through knowing and caring for her. As Erin talked more about her experience of motherhood in her interview, she told me that, 'Women, biologically, are more genetically predisposed to nurture in a far greater way, a different way from men.' She told me that she sees female nurturance as both a 'role' and a 'predisposition' and the bond between mother and child is doubly special because it is *both* 'natural' and 'social'.

Kirsty is a medical researcher in her thirties. At the time of our interview she had recently returned to full-time work following maternity leave. Her husband looks after their daughter full-time. This reversal of typical parental roles was unique among those I met during fieldwork. While most would approve of such arrangements, they assumed that mothers would usually act as the primary caregivers for children. Indeed, Kirsty told me that, if she could, she would have stayed at home with her daughter, but because her husband is disabled, it makes more financial sense for her to be the working parent in their family.

During the course of our interview, I asked Kirsty if she perceived differences between her and her husband's parenting styles. She said:

> I think that men and women approach parenthood differently in the time leading up to it. Women have the nine months where they're getting used to the idea – your body's being taken over by this parasite that you've got growing inside you. Men, although they kind of know what's going to happen, it doesn't really hit them between the eyes until the moment that the baby arrives and then, in our case, it was a bit of a shock to the system. He was like, 'oh my god, I'm a dad!', but in a good way.

> In our case, we approach parenthood in exactly the same way. We have pretty much the same views on what is the right or wrong thing to do. *The difference is that when my daughter cries, I have a physical reaction to it, not just an emotional reaction.* It's not quite so bad now she's a year old, but you can feel the hormone rush in response to the crying, which he doesn't have, so I respond more quickly and a little bit more anxiously, and he's a little bit more chilled out – but that's not a bad thing! I don't think other than that that we approach it any differently. (Emphasis added)

Kirsty was keen to emphasise what she and her husband share, which is the values they bring to parenthood, yet she nonetheless identified a difference in the physicality of her bond to their daughter, referring, like others, to the nine-month period of pregnancy to differentiate her experience as a parent and the bond with her daughter from her husband's, though she suggested this is an initial difference that will ultimately be evened out. While she used a physiological idiom for both of them, she perceived a different time span for the process of bonding, so while her body was 'taken over by this parasite' from conception, her husband was not physically 'hit ... between the eyes' by fatherhood until their daughter was born, which was a 'shock to the system'.

Erin saw motherhood as one of the most important and transformative experiences of her life. In particular, she described being 'hit with this massive responsibility, or a notion of responsibility, which just explodes when the child arrives'. Other interviewees also assumed that feeling such a close connection to her child would drive her mother to take ultimate responsibility for caring for and nurturing her. Given that they believed the maternal bond to be a natural phenomenon, it is perhaps unsurprising that most believed this would have an effect on how mothers and fathers cared for their children. This is demonstrated by Amy's comments. At the time of our interview, Amy was in her early thirties, single, did not have children and worked in environmental education. She told me:

> I think the mum has a stronger bond at the beginning, but I think that's just to do with carrying the baby around for nine months. But then, the dad seems to be kind of more doting and spoils the child a lot more sometimes. So, I think the mother – it's kind of stereotypical – but the mother always seems to be the more kind of practical one and does the basic care of the child, whereas the dad is usually the one that comes in and spoils the children and plays with them.

Interviewees were evenly split in whether they thought that a mother's bond to a child would be stronger or more 'special' than a father's throughout their child's life or if this difference would eventually even out. But, while people disagreed about how far-reaching the effects of the mother-child bond may be in time, they all assumed that the physical, hormonal and emotional realities of pregnancy and labour offer the right conditions for a 'special' relationship to grow between mother and child. Their repeated references to the nine-month gestation period show the significance of time in maternal bonding: while maternal bonding is set in motion by natural and physical processes, it must be nurtured to develop properly.

While they were supportive of gender equality, in talking about the maternal bond, the participants in my research foregrounded biologically determinist ideas of gender difference to make a claim for the specialness of motherhood. They saw this specialness as bringing rewards and costs. By associating the responsibilities of parenthood with the maternal bond, which is seen as being closely related to the physical intimacy of pregnancy and birth, it becomes both a biological and ethical expectation for a mother to form a close bond with her child and this has implications for the way in which parenthood is thought to properly impact on her life (see also Ginsburg 1989; Rapp 1999). Given the strong feelings of bonding which people expected to be generated during pregnancy and which shape the ensuing relationship between parent and child, what happens when pregnancy, bonding and parenting are separated between different women, as in surrogacy arrangements?

Surrogacy and the Maternal Bond

Although there are suggestions that informal surrogacy arrangements have always existed, surrogacy decisively entered the British public arena in the 1980s with the case of Kim Cotton, the UK's first, and so far only, 'commercial' surrogate mother. Cotton, a married mother of two, carried a baby on behalf of a Swedish couple who paid her £6500 in an arrangement organised by an American surrogacy agency working in southeast England, though in fact she received far more money for selling her story to a newspaper (Cotton & Winn 1985). Her case provoked a media storm and led to the hasty establishment of the Surrogacy Arrangements Act (Hansard 1985), which bans profit-making agencies from working as surrogacy 'brokers', the advertising of surrogacy services and the payment of compensation 'beyond reasonable expenses' by intended parents to surrogate mothers.

Cannell (1990: 674) has argued that Cotton was a culturally problematic figure because she had failed to bond with the child she carried as a surrogate. Despite the fact that she was thereby fulfilling the obligation she had made to the intended parents, in the contemporary uproar, her actions came to represent quintessentially 'bad' and 'unnatural' maternal behaviour. Maternal bonding is crucial in people's judgements about surrogacy because it is both a template for good feminine and maternal behaviour and a concept in which, as Cannell says, the moral and biological seem to be fused in one relationship.

Surrogacy disturbs normative ideas of maternal bonding, maternal responsibility and more widely, feminine behaviour, because a surrogate is supposed, and in some sense morally obliged, to relinquish the child she has borne to someone else's care. With surrogacy, the expectation that a pregnant woman will naturally 'bond' with the child she is carrying collides with her obligation to uphold her bond of trust[4] to the intended parents. This exposes the fact that maternal bonding may not be as natural and automatic as might be assumed. However, if a surrogate mother does bond with the child she is carrying, she will find it difficult, or perhaps impossible, to relinquish her to the intended parents. Thinking about maternal bonding from the perspective of surrogacy is, therefore, an opportunity to examine and explore the nature, and the naturalness, of the maternal bond more carefully and I turn now to what the participants in my research thought about maternal bonding in surrogacy.

Fiona, a divorced teacher in her fifties with one adult daughter, was generally pro-surrogacy. She was, however, concerned that a surrogate would find it difficult to hand over a baby and saw this as the greatest risk for all parties to a surrogacy arrangement. She said:

> I know that I could never have handed over a baby that I had borne. I would find that completely impossible, and that's not a rational decision based on any kind of belief, I just simply couldn't do it. . . . Some women don't have nearly such a strong maternal sense. To me, it would be like cutting off my hand, I couldn't do it.

Luke, a graduate student in his late twenties with no children, described the bond between a surrogate mother and child in a very similar manner to that used by others to describe the bond between a conventional mother and child:

> I can fully understand the attachment after having gone through all the process of having the baby growing inside you must, you can't shut yourself off from that, you can't treat it like it's a job, so I can understand the emotional attachment. . . . It must be very natural for a mother to want to keep the baby.

Luke suggests that it is natural that a surrogate should form a bond with the child she has carried, so it would be unnatural for her to 'reject' this bond by relinquishing her to her intended mother. Yet, to do so would be to abrogate her obligations towards the intended parents.

Roughly half of the interviewees interpreted the hypothetical 'nightmare scenario' of a surrogate mother refusing to relinquish the child as a question of whether the child was, in fact, 'hers' (cf. Warnock 1985: 47). Nina said quite bluntly, 'Well, it's not her baby, is it? . . . Biologically, it's not hers. I mean, she's [just] carried it'.[5] Nina's assumption that gestational surrogacy, where the surrogate carries a foetus which has been conceived from the intended parents' gametes using IVF, was the most common form of surrogacy suggests a desire to minimise the more culturally problematic aspects of surrogacy. In fact in the UK among heterosexual intended parents it is not as common as 'traditional surrogacy', in which the surrogate is artificially inseminated with the intended father's sperm.

Andrew, a conservation volunteer in his mid-twenties who had no children, also argued that a gestational surrogate who lacks a genetic link with the child would have a less valid claim to motherhood:

> I think that, while the nine month period is very, very important, I don't think that, if she doesn't have any genetic link and she's been aware from the first instance that it was almost a business relationship – and I'd imagine they'd sign contracts these days, anyway – I don't think I would grant custody [to the surrogate] if I were a judge in that situation.

Surrogacy contracts are legally unenforceable in the UK, which prioritises the gestational mother's claim to parenthood until a Parental Order has been issued transferring parental rights to the intended parents. Britain has therefore experienced a small number of legal cases concerning surrogacy. In the fairly recent case of *TT (a minor)* ([2011] EWHC 33 (*Fam*)), a British judge found in favour of a surrogate mother who claimed the baby she had carried for the intended parents as hers. Mr Justice Baker summed up his position, saying, '[the] natural process of carrying and giving birth to a baby creates an attachment which may be so strong that the surrogate mother finds herself unable to give up the child' (quoted in Gamble & Ghevaert 2011). Interestingly, in his judgement, the judge did not refer to the fact that the surrogate was a 'traditional' surrogate and therefore genetically related to the child she had carried, but focused instead on the 'attachment' created by the 'natural process' of pregnancy and labour, implying, in line with Fiona and Luke's judgements, that this in itself is a sufficient basis upon which to claim motherhood.

Luke and Fiona expected a surrogate mother to form a bond with the child because the maternal bond arises naturally out of the embodied experience of pregnancy. According to this reasoning, it is logically difficult to refute either a traditional or gestational surrogate mother's claim to the child since, as Luke said, 'it must be very natural for a mother to want to keep the baby'. Nina and Andrew, meanwhile, claimed that the maternal bond comes from genetic kinship, so it would be impossible to deny a traditional surrogate's claim to motherhood, while gestational surrogacy is acceptable as the intended mother's claim represents a more comfortable balance of both biological and social motherhood. In making these distinct claims, each set of participants draws on the concept of the maternal bond as a natural – and therefore given – phenomenon.[6]

A Natural Feeling

The idea that a surrogate mother might decide to assert parental rights over the child she has carried for the intended parents was often expressed by interviewees as a 'change of mind', based on the assumption that feelings of attachment to the child might 'kick in', causing her to feel that she was, after all, her mother. In talking about surrogacy and maternal bonding, interviewees often mentioned feelings and emotion. They described emotions as physical, embodied experience and the maternal bond as a feeling of attachment that compels a mother to respond to her child appropriately.

When I talked to Lizzy, a student in her late teens without children, about surrogacy, she mentioned that a friend of hers has once offered to act as a surrogate in the future for a mutual gay male friend of theirs if he ever decided to have children. Lizzy told me she admired her friend's generosity, but explained that she would not be able to do it herself: 'I am a very emotional person and I am not sure if I would be able to cope emotionally being a surrogate mother', she said, before adding, 'after going through the emotional rollercoaster of having a child and then to give it to someone else even if that was already established beforehand, I don't think I would be able to do it'.

Many believed that some process of psychological assessment would be appropriate before a surrogacy arrangement was set up, suggesting that counselling should be provided to the parties involved (but especially the surrogate mother), not only to provide emotional support but also as a means of vetting potential surrogates by weeding out those who are not emotionally fit for the role (see also Hirsch 1993). This idea that the assessment of a potential surrogate's psychological state may act as a competent measure of her fitness for the role is commensurate with British clinical practice, as surrogates and intended parents are expected to attend repeated counselling sessions throughout the entire process (Brinsden 2003). By insisting that the surrogate be emotionally strong, in itself a difficult thing to measure, people implicitly set limits on surrogacy's availability.

The participants in my research agreed that 'altruism', or feelings of love and sympathy towards the intended parents, was the best motivator for a surrogate mother but the vast majority also believed that surrogate mothers are entitled to receive some payment for their service. As Cannell has pointed out, if surrogates can claim to be *motivated* by altruism towards the intended parents, even if they are also paid, then it may be easier to frame their behaviour as acceptable within wider cultural ideologies of femininity (see Almeling 2011 for some parallel ideas in egg and sperm donation).

In her classic study of commercial surrogacy arrangements in the USA, Ragoné (1994) observed that intended parents are encouraged to nurture their surrogates, thereby cultivating feelings of attachment between them in order to make their obligation to relinquish the child when she is born all the more compelling. The participants in my research assumed that if she were motivated by altruism then a surrogate would feel better about what she had done, because she could emphasise her motivation to help someone over the fact that she had 'failed' to form a maternal bond and 'given up' a child. For those who were in favour of surrogacy, the surrogate's 'unnatural' relinquishing of the child she has carried is obviated by her altruistic act of helping another, with whom she has, or has come to form, a bond of sisterhood or friendship that can replace the bond she might have formed with the child. In the British context, which prohibits payment of the surrogate mother, this could also provide a 'reward' for the surrogate mother.

As Lutz (1988) has argued, emotions confound the Cartesian splitting of mind and body, because they are thought to originate in the mind but be felt in the body. Because they are seen in Western cultures as arising out of an individual's particular psyche, their social nature is rarely appreciated. As Lutz (1988: 4) argues, we need to recognise that emotions are as much an index of social relations as external manifestations of individuals' inner states. As this case of people speculating about the emotional state and drives of surrogate mothers shows, the language of emotions is an important clue to wider ethical values and 'structures of feeling' (Williams 1977). The example of surrogacy also reminds us that ideas about motive and human nature are gendered – women are expected to be naturally compelled towards altruism and this is exemplified by motherhood.

Another important point made by Lutz is that emotions are strongly associated with nature and biology, which makes them appear given and inescapable. Here, when people talked about the emotional strength of the surrogate mother, they were not only connecting mind and body through the language of emotions, but also talking about nature. The concerns people expressed to me about the consequences of a surrogate forming a bond with the child and her emotional state, particularly at the moment of postpartum handover, show the cultural and moral significance of this defining act in the surrogacy arrangement. Surrogacy is troubling because the surrogate is expected to resist a natural feeling that is supposed to be so strong and compelling that refuting it would be emotionally damaging.

Conclusion

Surrogacy is interesting to social scientists precisely because, in the debates that surround it, norms of motherhood, femininity and kinship become, in Strathern's (1992a) terms, 'literalised', by which she means they are exposed to active attention, which can have the knock-on effect of making them seem less certain because they appear made rather than given. The ethical dilemmas provoked by surrogacy demonstrate that motherhood is heavily laden with moral values which inscribe expectations for proper behaviour and relationships and which are articulated in the language of nature, genetics, biology and embodied feeling. Any challenge to maternal bonding, like the relinquishing of a child by a surrogate mother, seems to represent a threat to our most basic relationship and source of identity.

The data presented here demonstrate that, for the participants in my research, the maternal bond is a natural phenomenon with powerful effects for understandings of kinship and gender and the organisation of parenting. It shows that maternal bonding, while 'natural', needs to be worked on. Putting time, care and effort into bonding with their children is the primary act of maternal labour and responsibility. As I have shown, maternal bonding is not a rigid ideology but one that encompasses a range of both given and made aspects. Nonetheless, its naturalness was never questioned – for the people I interviewed in Scotland, the maternal bond can still be 'natural' whether it is based in gestational or genetic kinship. Nature has long been associated with automatic and instinctual behaviours, but, as this special issue argues, it is also a concept with great ethical force and moral authority in the contemporary Western world. It is little wonder, then, that the idea of maternal bonding has such potency.

While the maternal bond is a particularly robust concept, participants in my research disagreed about its specific form and effects. They did not suggest that fathers lack a connection with their children, nor did they doubt that intended parents in surrogacy arrangements would bond with their children, but they did assume that mothers who have carried and given birth to children experience a qualitatively different – or 'special' – bond. They differed on whether this is an initial difference or a more long-term one. Similarly, while this difference was closely associated with the physical experience of maternity, they emphasised various aspects of this, including pregnancy, labour, breast-feeding and responses to the sound of a child crying.

The maternal bond informs expectations about mothers' different responsibilities and identities in all spheres of life. Locating its initiation in the pregnant woman marks off motherhood as special, unique and somewhat mysterious. This provides mothers with rewarding feelings of attachment to their children and access to a highly valued status, but the idea of the 'nine-month head-start' has significant ramifications for how parental labour is organised. The term 'bond' encompasses notions of physical constraint and obligation as well as emotional attachment. Good mothering is thought to entail self-sacrifice, selflessness and a strong sense of responsibility; this is compelled by the feelings of attachment that women are expected to form with their children from pregnancy onwards. It, therefore, seems 'natural' that mothers will also be the primary caregivers of children, because they feel physically and emotionally compelled to do so by their bonds with their children.

For the participants in my research, the surrogate mother epitomised the anomalous and ethically fraught nature of surrogacy and talking about her 'unnatural' act of rejecting a child she had borne made their ideas about maternal bonding and motherhood explicit. While surrogacy seems on the one hand to challenge fundamental values and axioms of kinship and parenting, it also causes people to reproduce normative ideas about the nature and ethic of motherhood.

Disclosure statement

No potential conflict of interest was reported by the author.

Notes

1. I use the term 'maternal bond' rather than 'maternal-infant bond' or 'mother-child bond' throughout the article to reflect the fact that interviewees typically discussed bonding from the point of view of the mother or surrogate mother's feelings towards the child, rather than a reciprocal attachment between mother and child. Furthermore, none of them speculated on whether the child would bond to a surrogate mother.
2. Of course the particular ideas about motherhood and surrogacy discussed here are located in a particular socio-economic milieu. Not only are the participants in my research middle-class, but it is generally assumed that assisted conception including surrogacy is most commonly sought by middle- and upper-class intended parents. Though it is difficult to get accurate figures on this, there is some evidence to suggest that, at least in commercial surrogacy, surrogates are more likely to be working class than intended parents (see Ragoné 1994). Furthermore, while the public debate around surrogacy crosses class and party political boundaries, on

the whole, the most influential figures in terms of policy have been lawyers, journalists and ethicists. This is reflected in much of the anthropological work on assisted conception, with the notable exception of Edwards' (2000) work in Lancashire.
3. See also Strathern (2003; 1992b) for a discussion of whether the ethical dilemmas presented by surrogacy are as novel as they might at first appear.
4. Of course, the word 'bond' has a further, financially inflected meaning, which is worth bearing in mind given the contentious debate over commercial surrogacy.
5. Notably, when talking about her own reproductive plans as quoted in the previous section, Nina emphasised the importance of experiencing pregnancy, yet with surrogate motherhood she sidelines gestation.
6. Markens (2007) carried out a comparative study of surrogacy regulation in the states of New York and California. Of particular relevance to my analysis here is Markens' focus on 'discursive frames' in the debates in each state. In both New York and California, both pro- and anti-surrogacy camps referred to 'the best interests of the child' and the 'freedom to choose' in making opposing arguments (see Edwards *et al.* 1993 for some parallels in the British debates around assisted conception in the 1980s and Ginsburg 1989 on the American abortion debate). Similarly, the participants in my research appealed to apparently stable concepts of genetics, biology and nature, but to make different and in some cases contradictory claims.

References

Almeling, Rene. 2011. *Sex Cells: The Medical Market for Eggs and Sperm*. London: University of California Press.
Anderson, Elizabeth S. 1990. Is Women's Labor a Commodity? *Philosophy and Public Affairs*, 19(1):71–92.
Brinsden, Peter R. 2003. Clinical Aspects of IVF Surrogacy in Britain. In *Surrogate Motherhood: International Perspectives*, edited by Rachel Cook, Shelley Day Sclater & Felicity Kaganas. pp. 99–116. Oxford: Hart Publishing.
Cannell, Fenella. 1990. Concepts of Parenthood: The Warnock Report, the Gillick Debate and Modern Myths. *American Ethnologist*, 17(4):667–686.
Cook, Rachel, Shelley Day Sclater & Felicity Kaganas (eds.). 2003. *Surrogate Motherhood: International Perspectives*. Oxford: Hart Publishing.
Cooper, Melinda & Catherine Waldby. 2014. *Clinical Labor: Tissue Donors and Research Subjects in the Global Bioeconomy*. London: Duke University Press.
Corea, Gena. 1985. *The Mother Machine: Reproductive Technologies from Artificial Insemination to Artificial Wombs*. New York: Harper and Row.
Cotton, Kim & Denise Winn. 1985. *Baby Cotton: For Love and Money*. London: Dorling Kindersley.
Davis, Kelly. 2008. *'Here's Your Baby, on You Go': Kinship and Expert Advice Amongst Mothers in Scotland* (Unpublished PhD thesis). University of Edinburgh, Edinburgh.
Dow, Katharine. 2013. Building a Stable Environment in Scotland: Planning Parenthood in a Time of Ecological Crisis. In *Parenting in Global Perspective: Negotiating Ideologies of Kinship, Self and Politics*, edited by Charlotte Faircloth, Diane M. Hoffman & Linda L. Layne. London: Routledge.
Drummond, Lee. 1978. The Transatlantic Nanny: Notes on a Comparative Semiotics of the Family in English-Speaking Societies. *American Ethnologist*, 5(1):30–43.

Edwards, Jeanette. 2000. *Born and Bred: Idioms of Kinship and New Reproductive Technologies in England.* Oxford: Oxford University Press.

Edwards, Jeanette, Sarah Franklin, Eric Hirsch, Frances Price & Marilyn Strathern (eds.). 1993. *Technologies of Procreation: Kinship in the age of assisted conception.* Manchester: Manchester University Press.

Eyer, Diane E. 1992. *Mother-infant Bonding: A Scientific Fiction.* New Haven, CT: Yale University Press.

Faircloth, Charlotte. 2013. *Militant Lactivism: Attachment Parenting and Intensive Motherhood in the UK and France.* Oxford: Berghahn.

Faircloth, Charlotte, Diane M. Hoffman & Linda L. Layne (eds.). 2013. *Parenting in Global Perspective: Negotiating Ideologies of Kinship, Self and Politics.* London: Routledge.

Franklin, Sarah. 2013. *Biological Relatives: IVF, Stem Cells, and the Future of Kinship.* London: Duke University Press.

Gamble, Natalie & Louisa Ghevaert. 2011. Surrogacy, Parenthood and Disputes: Are There Any Lessons to be Learned? *BioNews,* p. 595.

Ginsburg, Faye. 1989. *Contested Lives: The Abortion Debate in an American Community.* London: University of California Press.

Hansard. 1985. *Surrogacy Arrangements Act 1985.* London: HMSO.

Hays, Sharon. 1996. *The Cultural Contradictions of Motherhood.* New Haven, CT: Yale University Press.

Hirsch, Eric. 1993. Negotiated Limits: Interviews in South-East England. In *Technologies of Procreation: Kinship in the Age of Assisted Conception,* edited by Jeanette Edwards, Sarah Franklin, Eric Hirsch, Frances Price & Marilyn Strathern. pp. 67–95. Manchester: Manchester University Press.

Konrad, Monica. 2005. *Nameless Relations: Anonymity, Melanesia and Reproductive Gift Exchange between British Ova Donors and Recipients.* Oxford: Berghahn Books.

Lee, Ellie, Jennie Bristow, Charlotte Faircloth & Jan McVarish. 2014. *Parenting Culture Studies.* Basingstoke: Palgrave Macmillan.

Lutz, Catherine A. 1988. *Unnatural Emotions: Everyday Sentiments on a Micronesian Atoll and Their Challenge to Western Theory.* Chicago, IL: University of Chicago Press.

Markens, Susan. 2007. *Surrogate Motherhood and the Politics of Reproduction.* Berkeley: University of California Press.

Pande, Amrita. 2009. Not an "Angel", not a "Whore": Surrogates as "Dirty" Workers in India. *Indian Journal of Gender Studies,* 16:141–173.

———. 2010. "At Least I am Not Sleeping with Anyone": Resisting the Stigma of Commercial Surrogacy in India. *Feminist Studies,* 36(2):292–312.

Ragoné, Helena. 1994. *Surrogate Motherhood: Conception in the Heart.* Oxford: Westview Press.

Rapp, Rayna. 1999. *Testing Women, Testing the Fetus: The Social Impact of Amniocentesis in America.* New York, NY: Routledge.

Roberts, Elizabeth F. S. 1998. 'Native' Narratives of Connectedness: Surrogate Motherhood and Technology. In *Cyborg Babies: From Techno Sex to Techno-Tots,* edited by Robbie Davis-Floyd & Joseph Dumit. pp. 193–211. New York: Routledge.

Stanworth, Michelle (ed.). 1987. *Reproductive Technologies: Gender, Motherhood and Medicine.* Cambridge: Polity Press.

Strathern, Marilyn. 1992a. *After Nature: English Kinship in the Late Twentieth Century.* Cambridge: Cambridge University Press.
———. 1992b. *Reproducing the Future: Essays on Anthropology, Kinship, and the New Reproductive Technologies.* Manchester: Manchester University Press.
———. 2003. Still Giving Nature a Helping Hand? Surrogacy: A Debate about Technology and Society. In *Surrogate Motherhood: International Perspectives*, edited by R. Cook, S. D. Sclater & F. Kaganas. pp. 281–296. Oxford: Hart Publishing.
Suizzo, Marie-Anne. 2004. Mother-Child Relationships in France: Balancing Autonomy and Affiliation in Everyday Interactions. *Ethos*, 32(3):293–323.
Teman, Elly. 2003. 'Knowing' the Surrogate Body in Israel. In *Surrogate Motherhood: International Perspectives*, edited by Rachel Cook, Shelley Day Sclater & Felicity Kaganas. pp. 261–280. Oxford: Hart Publishing.
———. 2010. *Birthing a Mother: The Surrogate Body and the Pregnant Self.* London: University of California Press.
Thompson, Charis. 2001. Strategic Naturalizing: Kinship in an Infertility Clinic. In *Relative Values: Reconfiguring Kinship Studies*, edited by Sarah Franklin and Susan McKinnon. pp. 175–202. Durham, NC: Duke University Press.
———. 2005. *Making Parents: The Ontological Choreography of Reproductive Technologies.* London: The MIT Press.
Wall, Glenda. 2001. Moral Constructions of Motherhood in Breastfeeding Discourse. *Gender and Society*, 15(4):592–610.
Warnock, Mary. 1985. *A Question of Life: The Warnock Report on Human Fertilisation and Embryology.* Oxford: Blackwell.
Williams, Raymond. 1977. *Marxism and Literature.* Oxford: Oxford University Press.
Zipper, Juliette & Selma Sevenhuijsen. 1987. Surrogacy: Feminist Notions of Motherhood Reconsidered. In *Reproductive Technologies: Gender, Motherhood and Medicine*, edited by M. Stanworth. pp. 118–138. Cambridge: Polity Press.

A Response to the Issues Raised in the Special Edition of *Ethnos*

Alana Jelinek

ABSTRACT *An artist's response to the issues raised in the special edition of* Ethnos. *Using her own artwork to think through the issues raised, this afterword focuses on Levinas and a discussion around ethics and politics in both the artworld and anthropology. It ends with a discussion about storytelling or knowledge-formation and how Nature today serves the same rhetorical and narrative purpose that God has served in previous generations.*

This afterword creates a form of symmetry: the edition begins with art, *I wanna deliver a shark* by Ai Hasegawa and its challenge to nature and the ethics of both consumption and production, embodying the issues raised in this special edition of *Ethnos* and, with my afterword, it ends with an artist's response, thinking about the issues raised here through my own art practice. My practice engages directly with the main themes of this edition, namely ethics and nature. For the London artworld, not only does ethics contain the double meaning elaborated by Michael Lambek, as described in Adam Reed's contribution in this edition, but the positive meaning of the term has been synonymous with 'political' since the turn of the millennium. In the London artworld, the two concepts of ethics and politics are conveniently and knowingly intertwined. The term 'ethics' came to replace 'politics' when politics lost its lustre in the thrusting new world of the booming 1990s London art market. Arguably its recent centrality was a response to the perceived apolitics of 1980s and 1990s 'young British art' combined with the continuing need to disavow the old-fashioned concept of politics (Bishop 2006a; 2006b). Nevertheless, it would be misleading to characterise the artworld as having experienced an 'ethical turn' akin to that described by the contributors to this edition, as this phrase does not appear in the literature, unlike other 'turns'. Interestingly, the term 'politics' remains implicit in most of the contributions to this special edition.

I write from the perspective of London and, though the art market is global as are many instances of contemporary art practice, I do not claim universality when I write of the artworld. My analysis and comments are thoroughly grounded in the London artworld, its discourses, politics and economic structures.

Ethics in its other sense, meaning the general field in which criteria for human interaction are explored, is less a prevailing concern for the artworld than ethics as politics. Work that reflects on the general field includes Artur Żmijewski (for example, *80064* a film in which the faded ID-number of an Auschwitz survivor is re-tattooed onto the perhaps un-consenting aged survivor, 2005), Santiago Sierra (for example, *160 cm Line Tattooed on 4 People El Gallo Arte Contemporáneo. Salamanca, Spain. December 2000*, a photograph of a live art event at which four prostitutes addicted to heroin were hired for the price of a shot of heroin to have a line tattooed across their backs) and my own work, particularly *The Field* (2008–ongoing) which I have described as an art experiment in Levinasian ethics (Jelinek & Brown 2014). Sierra and Żmijewski foreground ethics by working in a negative ethical register which is assumed to be at odds with that of their audience. *The Field*, by contrast, is an attempt at engaging the other as Other thereby reflecting and contributing to the general field.

The Field is a 12.9 acre area of ancient woodland and meadow in Essex, England on the boundary of a once-grand estate. It is a location for art, conservation and outreach projects, but it is more than the mere physical host for such activities. In itself, *The Field* is a long-term, participatory, interspecies art project. It is a physical, geographical location at a specific moment in time with a set of ethical and aesthetic propositions attached. It is hoped that *The Field* affords participants the opportunity to engage mindfully and reflexively in relationships with other humans and other non-human species, both plant and animal. Behind it lies the philosophy of Emmanuel Levinas and his observation that Western knowledge (philosophy) has been based on an assumption and an alarming paradox: that knowledge is universal, while knowledge stems from, and is confined to, the particularity of the Greco-European experience and tradition. Levinas understands that knowledge, based on this *philia*, a system of likeness, on the exchange of the same with the same, is a system of knowledge, of thought, of culture that inherently has a horror of the Other. This horror can only be minimised when the Other is assimilated as part of the same. The Other is not allowed to be other; it must be an extension of the self or the same (Critchley 1992: 31). Orientalism, primitivism and, in the case of animals, anthropomorphism can be understood as cultural manifestations of the extension of the self.

Levinas had informed my thinking, artwork and curating of exhibitions prior to *The Field*. Despite being a Talmudic scholar, his ethics are not predicated on religion. They seem extraordinarily secular given his commitment to Judaic thought. His ethics do not refer to morality. They are not about being a better person or having more empathy. Empathy suggests an imaginative leap which reduces the Other to the Same: the violence of 'we' (Hutchens 2004). Known for his metaethics, to my mind Levinas's ethics is fundamentally epistemological: we cannot know another and therefore we cannot reliably assume anything about them. Indeed, others cannot know ourselves and we cannot expect them to act as if they have this knowledge. For Levinas, we must always act and think with respect to the unknowableness of the other and is only when we act accordingly that we can have ethical engagements.

When I first encountered the work of contemporary anthropologists, I was struck by some of the disciplinary similarities with fine art practice, specifically anthropology's self-reflexivity. There were a number of philosophers that both disciplines read: Foucault in particular and Haraway. What surprised me was the absence of Levinas. To me, anthropology is all about the ethics of engaging with others as Other and yet it seems Levinas has made but a modest impression. (That said, he is name-checked but not unpacked by Adam Reed.) What is stranger perhaps is that he is often cited within the artworld, a discipline not particularly interested in ethics qua ethics.

For Levinas, any other, any other person is other as unknowably Other. I have somewhat misappropriated his work, stretching his understanding to make sense of my relationships with other cultures and engage ethically in my exploration of colonialism and neocolonialism. *The Field* is a further discourtesy to his intentions, especially in its inclusion of the non-human.

In reading the ethnographies presented in this edition of *Ethnos*, I am reminded of my own journey via *The Field* around the concept of Nature. It was both the experience of working on *The Field* and working with anthropologists that has shifted my understanding of the Nature–Culture divide. At the beginning of the project in 2008, I had considered Art, Science, Religion, subjects one studies at school and university and all man-made things (material and non-material) as culture. All else was nature. It was with this frame that I approached the field site. Despite being on the perimeter of a once-grand country estate, all I could see was trees and birds, none of which I could identify. These, I understood, as Nature and I felt self-conscious about inserting culture, that is Art, into the context despite (or because of) a history of Land Art also informing the project. I could not see that, despite the woodland's ancientness, the majority of trees had been planted by the landowners who once lived there, being coppiced hornbeam and hawthorn, interspersed by oak standards and a line of cherry laurel used possibly as cover for game birds. I did not know then that the Romans brought rabbits to Britain (so in my view culture, not nature) or that both roe and fallow deer were brought to Britain by subsequent rulers. I thought they belonged and so they were nature. If they were brought by man, they become culture in my personal taxonomy. I was so self-conscious about the nature–culture divide, the first allotments we drew up were in the shapes of Islamic tiles; being based in maths Islamic tile patterns are therefore, to my mind, Culture writ large.

I recognise the place of an Abrahamic God in this concept of Nature and, I would argue, God is present in all the ethnographies presented here in this edition of *Ethnos*. This is not to say that Nature and God are the same thing in anyone's mind, least of all the informants in these ethnographies, but that Nature has replaced the concept of God in its capacity to act as a baseline or universal reference point. Just as we need(ed) the concept of God so we invented him, we need the concept of Nature. But my point goes deeper than this. I wish to consider the idea of how knowledge is formed, to consider how we collect and frame our knowledge, as all knowledge, in my view, is ultimately storytelling.

Demonstrating this idea in 2013, I wrote and published a novel from the point of view of an object in a museum's collection. The novel was an attempt at exploring the idea of collections and collecting from the naive but not unintelligent position of an object that has been collected. In addition to the various observations about living and historical collectors and the historical facts about the object narrating the stories, the novel explored the idea of the 'ambient ether', which I conceived as the stories that comprise discourse in any one place and at any one time. In the novel, *The Fork's Tale, as Narrated by Itself* (Jelinek 2013), I gave discourse substance, making it another set of things that a collector will collect, both substantial and part of the ether. All humans were conceived therefore as collectors in that all humans collect stories and things.

Through *The Fork's Tale*, I began to explore the idea that all forms of collecting, including collections of knowledge or storytelling, are based on previous patterns of collecting. By the time I came to write it, I had already begun to look at knowledges and storytelling, how some people choose to collect and pass on one type of knowledge or stories while others pick up different ones even when they are exposed to a wide range. From 2010 until 2012, I worked with colleagues at the Museum of Archaeology and Anthropology, University of Cambridge, to explore what they understood they knew about the Fijian 'cannibal forks' in the collection. I listened to and collected knowledge from a wide range of people, including anthropologists and scholars as well as front of house staff and museum technicians (*Tall Stories: Cannibal Forks 2010, 2012*). What was interesting to me was not so much the truth of the stories (I continue to believe this is an impossible quest), but the types of stories recollected by different people. It was clear to me that knowledge, the stories we choose to seek out and pass on, is a kind of self-portrait. We are, all of us, exposed to a wide range of stories, but only some are retained, recollected and distributed.

I am an atheist, like many involved with *The Field*, but I am not a secularist, unlike most. I like religion and I accept it as part of our deeply embedded storytelling and therefore our knowledge traditions. I can see how, for me, Nature means/meant what God put there, as distinct from what Man does and I think like this despite being an atheist. There are stories and ways of narrating that have deep roots and these form schema onto which other knowledge is placed. Knowledge here includes ideas about Nature, both scientific and lay. That evolution is understood as progress even by some evolutionary biologists is, I would argue, an artefact of the Abrahamic religions. There is nothing inherent in the concept of evolution that requires this teleological flavour, the understanding of evolution as progress towards something (that something being Man). Nevertheless, evolution by natural selection resonates with ideas of progress because, I would argue, it has been overlaid on a schema created from older forms of storytelling, those derived from stories of progress from darkness to light and chaos to Man. Thomas (1991) describes how ideas and projects of precolonial cultures are a significant factor in the success or failures of the various aspects of the colonial project. I would argue similarly, that knowledge (stories) only has salience when it is overlaid on schema that already exist and that this operates on both an individual level and a societal one. It is a deep storytelling, a way of organising stories, stemming from the Abrahamic religions at the heart of Western culture that informs how knowledge is arranged and framed in the West (for want of a better term).

The idea that Nature means what God put there as distinct from what Man does also pervades the thinking of Adam Reed's informants. There is Man and there is everything else. Man is a special case in the world. Further, not only is Man a special case, different from all other animals, but Man is bad: a concept as familiar as Original Sin. Again in common with Christianity, they offer a way to overcome the badness of man: we must be more in touch with our in-born natures, like children. Nature and God are seemingly interchangeable at the level of schema, though not interchangeable as overt content. The content is clearly (and perhaps avowedly) secular. The fact that the animal protection informants evangelise, believing it is both possible and proper to convert others to their way of thinking, further evidences the existence of narrative artefacts derived from other, older forms of storytelling and knowledge-formation. This contrasts with the informants of both Katharine Dow and Charlotte Faircloth who are slightly different in their relationship to Nature. They both share a reliance on Nature and evolution as the most correct baseline informing their decisions about how to live. Instead of being written in the stars or in God's heart, our behaviours and identities are predestined by genes. Structured like this we can see how older stories about an Abrahamic God serve as placeholders for their concepts of nature and evolution. Adherence to what is natural, adherence to Nature, is charged with moral authority because it is God (-like). When Dow and Boydell observe in the introduction to this special issue that 'in contemporary Britain, nature seems also to have become laden with moral authority and ethical potency', I would argue that this is because Nature has replaced God in a form of storytelling that has deep roots. It is this elision of God with Nature that accounts perhaps for some of the concept's polysemy. It may also account for Nature's resistance to 'flattening' despite modern hybrid monsters and technology.

Mascha Gugganig's writing about genetic engineering (GE) of taro in Hawaii elucidates Nature as God from a different angle. Native Hawaiians are, in general, Christian but their Christianity is nuanced with a Polynesian sense of w*hakapapa*. Nature is a concept differently understood by those without Hawaiian w*hakapapa*. As humans born of *Haloa* born of *Ho'ohokukalani* they are definitely part of Nature: no exceptionalism. Reading this paper piqued my own sense of transgression around GE. Though I do not share the sacredness of understanding that accompanies those with *whakapapa*, I realise that I too have a sense of God in Nature with regard species-specific DNA. I realise that it is vitally important to me to preserve the distinctions between the building blocks of different families or orders, if not species. I am well aware of the argument that GE is for the left what Climate Science is to the right, that its rejection will mean the needless death of countless millions, nevertheless there is something visceral in my feelings of rejection which I believe I recognise in the informants of Gugganig. That *something* seems close to a faith in the Natural Order of Things, or God by another name. Of course, for those on the left, there is also the issue of trust in corporations and systems of privatised knowledge (patents) neither of which have traditionally been associated with the common good. Nevertheless it is the very depth of abject feeling towards GE that alerts me to something else going on. I envy the Native Hawaiian their rhetorical, moral and political authority to end the experiments on Hawaiian taro.

I must highlight and own some of the differences between my discipline, fine art practice, and that of the assumed readership of this journal, anthropology. Having worked with anthropologists for the past six years through my research with the Museum of Archaeology & Anthropology, University of Cambridge, and having contributed to anthropology journals and therefore having been subject to readers' comments from anthropologists, I am aware that my writing might inspire frustration in some. For some readers, as this is not anthropology, it must be the writing of an informant. In anthropology, knowledge is created through a process in which numbers of informants are brought together and their testaments compared in the hope that trends emerge and singularities noted but dismissed. All informants are treated with equal scepticism and equal respect. This is not true of either critical writing within fine art practice or within history of art. Here, knowledge is created in reference to others who write or make art and rests on a bedrock of acknowledged experts. I would argue that anthropology works analogously at the theoretical end of the spectrum; a point illustrated here in contributors' references to Strathern, Ingold or Descola, for example. My hope in writing this afterword is that it is read, not as an informant writing from a singular point of view in need of contextualisation amongst others of my kind, but as one whose singularity is their contribution. I make no claims to having proven that knowledge or storytelling is a type of self-portrait or that Nature really has replaced all that the concept of God used to contain. As with any artist's contribution,

I simply offer these ideas here and these ideas may or may not resonate with my audience.

Disclosure statement

No potential conflict of interest was reported by the author.

References

Bishop, Claire (ed.). 2006a. *Participation*. London: Whitechapel Art Gallery.

———. 2006b. The Social Turn: Collaboration and Its Discontents. *Artforum*, 44(6):178–183.

Critchley, Simon. 1992. *The Ethics of Deconstruction: Derrida and Levinas*. Edinburgh: Edinburgh University Press.

Hutchens, B. C. 2004. *Levinas: A Guide for the Perplexed*. London: Continuum.

Jelinek, Alana. 2013. *The Fork's Tale, as Narrated by Itself*. London: LemonMelon.

Jelinek, Alana & Juliette Brown. 2014. The Field: An Art Experiment in Levinasian Ethics. In *Living Beings: Perspective on Interspecies Engagements*, edited by Penny Dransart. London: Bloomsbury.

Thomas, Nicholas. 1991. *Entangled Objects: Exchange, Material Culture, and Colonialism in the Pacific*. Cambridge, MA and London: Harvard University Press.

Index

Abram, S. 7
adaptation 20–1, 23, 28–30, 39
adoption 92
agency 11, 73, 78–9
Almeling, R. 99
altruism 98–9
Anderson, E. S. 90
animal protection 68–84, 110; animal–industrial complex 73; double meaning of 'ethical' 70; empathy 81–3; environmentalism vs 75–80; fox hunting the grouse 72–5; 'killing for fun' 73; reconnection 81–3; relative culpability 73; species interdependency 77; species survival and ecosystems 77, 80; (un)natural world 71–5; welfare of individual animals 77, 80
animal rights 14, 69, 70, 73, 77, 83; environmentalist ethics and 78–9
Anthropocene 8
anthropological theory and ethnography 4–10
anthropology of ethics 10–12
anthropomorphism 107
antibiotics 27
Ariès, P. 38
art practice 107, 111
artists 51, 105–12; Ai Hasegawa Ai 1–2, 14, 105
Atkinson, J. 6
attachment parenting 20, 21–3, 24, 25, 26, 27, 28, 29, 30, 32, 33, 34, 37, 38, 39, 40

attachment theory 22, 91
autonomy 36

Badinter, E. 21, 35, 37, 38
Bamford, S. 44, 45, 56, 58
Beckwith, W. M. 46
Bèkoff, M. 76, 78
Berglund, E. K. 7, 8, 77
Berkes, F. 44
biocolonialism 45
bio-piracy 44
bio-prospecting 45
biological diversity: Cartagena Protocol on Biosafety 45
biotechnology *see* genetic engineering and patenting
Bishop, C. 106
Bobel, C. 20, 21, 27, 28
branded clothes 27
breastfeeding 14, 19–40, 101, 110; accountability 22, 23, 26, 27, 28, 32; adaptation 20–1, 23, 28–30, 39; after-school and holiday club 32; attachment parenting 20, 21–3, 24, 25, 26, 27, 28, 29, 30, 32, 33, 34, 37, 38, 39, 40; attachment theory 22; context: parenting culture and feeding practices 21–4; 'corps erotique' 36; crèches/childcare 31–2, 34, 38; cross-cultural perspective: Paris 31–4; cycle of pregnancy and lactation 29; definition of full-term 25; ecological parenting 26–7, 34; empathy 29;

113

INDEX

employment 32; enslavement 33–4, 35–6; evolutionary parenting 26, 28–31, 34, 35, 40; flexibility 20–1, 28–9, 39; France: feminism and long-term 34–7; hominid blueprint of care 20, 28–9, 39; hunter–gathers 29–30, 38; identity work 22, 23, 25, 27, 30, 33, 37, 40; Internet 30, 33, 37; !Kung 30–1; language 29; maternity leave 31, 39; methods 24–5; paternity leave 31; pre-schools 32; public health policy 23, 32, 39; shifting orthodoxies 37; statistics 23
Brinsden, P. R. 98
Buskens, P. 21, 30, 38
Butler, J. 6
bycatch 75, 79

campaigning 82–3
Cannell, F. 95, 98–9
capitalism 27, 60
Carroll, Mele 50, 51
Cartagena Protocol on Biosafety 45
Cassidy, R. 9
childbirth 27, 29; *see also* maternal bond and surrogacy
childcare/crèches 31–2, 34, 38
Cho, J. 48
Choy, T. 7
class 3, 9, 22, 32, 35, 39, 87, 89
clothing 27
Collier, J. F. 5, 6
colonialism 107, 109; biocolonialism 45
companion animals/pets 74, 79, 83
compassionate conservation 78
context 11
contraception 26–7
Cook, R. 90
Cooper, M. 90
Corea, G. 90
Cotton, K. 95
counselling 98
Cram, F. 45
crèches/childcare 31–2, 34, 38
Critchley, S. 107
Cronon, W. 7, 8, 23
cross-cultural perspective: 'natural' breastfeeding with case studies in London and Paris *see* breastfeeding

Cruikshank, J. 44, 51
culling 79–80
Cummings, H. C. 44, 51

Davis, K. 91, 92–3
Dayton, K. 51
de Beauvoir, S. 36
death penalty 74
Descola, P. 4–5, 6, 7, 111
determinism 94–5
Dettwyler, K. 28, 39
disruptive event 83
double meaning of 'ethical' 70, 105
Dow, K. 7, 10, 91
Druckerman, P. 33
Drummond, L. 89
dualism 4–5

ecological parenting 26–7, 34
education and multinational companies 58, 60
Edwards, J. 9, 90
Einarsson, N. 9
Elle magazine 37
empathy 29, 81–3, 107
Engels, F. 38
Enlightenment 35, 37
Enos, Solomon 51
environmentalism 5, 7–8, 9–10, 51; animal protection vs 75–80
Essoyan, S. 49
evolution 109
evolutionary parenting 26, 28–31, 34, 35, 40
Eyer, D. E. 91

Faircloth, C. 20, 22, 23, 24, 26, 31, 32, 35, 89, 91
Faubion, J. D. 10, 11, 70
femininity 87, 90, 95, 99, 100
feminism 5–6, 21, 40; France: long-term breastfeeding and 34–7; surrogacy 90
The Field 106–8
fighting dogs 74
Fildes, V. 21
fine art practice 107, 111
Fitting, E. 44, 45
Fitzgerald, D. 5

INDEX

folk models 5, 6, 14
food: GE 56; organic 27, 37; sovereignty 60
fosterage 89
Foucault, M. 11, 70, 81, 107
France: 'natural' breastfeeding with case studies in London and Paris *see* breastfeeding
Franklin, S. 6, 7, 15, 20, 70, 90
freedom 11

Gamble, N. 97
Geertz, C. 59
gender 7, 9, 10, 90, 91, 100; determinism 94–5; division of labour 5–6, 14, 38–9, 89; motive and human nature 99
genetic engineering and patenting 14, 44–60, 110–11; apple snails 54; in the beginning, there was darkness 46–51; biosecurity 53; contested expertise 52–5, 59; corporations and education institutions 58–9, 60; cosmogenic creation story 46; cross-pollination 50; diseases affecting taro 46, 47–8, 49, 53, 54, 55; DNA mapping 53, 55; GE taro, the 'hybrid' 55–7; import laws 54; industrious objectivity 57–9; irrigation 53; kinship: Native Hawaiians and taro 45, 48, 50, 51–2, 57, 58, 59; Paoakalani Declaration (2003) 45, 48, 58; power relations 58, 59; resurgence of elder brother and ancestor 51–2; royalties 46; traditional knowledge 48, 56
Germany 8
Gima, C. 49
Ginsburg, F. 95
Goffman, E. 22
Gould, R. K. 6
green politics 14
Greene, S. 45, 58
Greer, F. N. 54
grouse and pheasant shoots *see* animal protection
Grove-White, R. 8

Hamilton, C. 50
Handy, C. S. E. 51, 53
Haraway, D. J. 14, 44, 58, 70, 71, 78–9, 84, 107

Hasegawa, Ai 1–2, 14, 105
Hashimoto, A. 48–9
Hastrup, K. 4, 13
Hausman, B. 28, 29, 30
Hawaii and taro (Colocasia esculenta) *see* genetic engineering and patenting
Hays, S. 23, 38, 89
He, X. 47, 48
Helm, A. 60
Hewlett, B. 29, 30, 39
Hirsch, E. 98
hominid blueprint of care 20, 28–9, 39
horses: Newmarket racing society 9
Howard, S. 45
Hrdy, S. 29, 30, 31, 38, 39
humanism 37
humans' relations with other animals 5, 8–10, 14, 106; animal protection *see separate entry*
Hume, D. 27
hunter–gathers 29–30, 38
Hutchens, B. C. 107
hybridity 46, 53, 55–7, 59

identity: breastfeeding and identity work 22, 23, 25, 27, 30, 33, 37, 40; national 37; politics 9; surrogacy and maternal bond 91, 100, 101
indigenous peoples 44–5; !Kung 30–1; Māori 45, 51, 57; Native Hawaiians and taro (Colocasia esculenta) *see* genetic engineering and patenting; United Nations Declaration on the Rights of 45
individualisation 3, 13
industrialisation 27
infertility clinics 89–90
Ing, K. M. 49
Ingold, T. 4, 111
intellectual property rights *see* genetic engineering and patenting
Internet 30, 33, 37

James, A. 6
Jasanoff, S. 44, 58, 60
Jelinek, A. 106, 108
judgement, practical 11

INDEX

Kame'eleihiwa, L. 46, 55
Keller, E. F. 6, 7
Kimbrell, A. 51
kinship 5, 6, 7, 14; kincentric ecology 51, 59; Native Hawaiians and taro 45, 48, 50, 51–2, 57, 58, 59; surrogacy and maternal bond 87, 89–90, 91, 97, 100, 101
knowledge 106–7, 108–10, 111
Kobayashi, C. 46–7, 49, 50
Konanui, J. 50, 51, 53
Konrad, M. 90
Kukla, R. 23
!Kung 30–1

LaDuke, W. 44, 45
Laidlaw, J. 10, 11, 69, 70, 73, 76
Lambek, M. 10, 11, 70, 105
language 29
Latour, B. 8, 46, 56, 58, 71, 84
Layne, L. 36–7
Lee, E. 22, 32, 89, 91
Leone, D. 48
Lévi-Strauss, C. 8–9
Levin, P. 50, 53, 54
Levinas, E. 83, 106–7
libertarianism 80
Lingle, Linda 51
Lo, C. 52, 55
lobbying 75–6, 78, 81, 83
Lovell, B. H. 55
Lutz, C. A. 99

MacCormack, C. 6, 20
Macnaghten, P. 6, 7
Maher, V. 31, 38
materialism 27
maternal bond and surrogacy 14, 95–8, 100–1, 110; altruism 98–9; contracts 97; counselling 98; femininity 87, 90, 95, 99, 100; identity 91, 100, 101; kinship 87, 89–90, 91, 97, 100, 101; natural feeling 98–100; nature of motherhood 88–91; 'nine-month head-start' 86–8, 91, 94, 101; vital difference 91–5
maternity leave 31, 39
menstruation 27
Mexico 45

middle class 3, 32, 35, 87, 89; parenting 22, 39
Milton, K. 7
Miyasaka, S. 47, 48, 54
modernism 14, 56
Monsanto 58
Moore, H. L. 6
Moorhead, A. 53
Moscucci, O. 27
mothering: breastfeeding *see separate entry*; maternal bond and surrogacy *see separate entry*
Mullin, M. H. 9
multinational companies 58–9, 60, 111
Murphy, E. 23
Myers Jr, O. E. 82

Nader, L. 44, 58, 59
nannies 89
nappies, cloth 27, 37
national identity 37
nationalism 60
Nelson, S. 46, 53, 54
neo-liberalism 57–8
New Zealand 45, 51

Orientalism 107
Ortner, S.B. 6
Osorio, Jonathan Kamakawiwoʻole 49
Ostrander, K. G. 49

Palmer, G. 31
Pande, A. 90
parenting: breastfeeding *see separate entry*; child-centred 89; *see also* maternal bond and surrogacy
patents *see* genetic engineering and patenting
paternity leave 31
pedigree pets 74
Perez, Andre 58
pets 74, 79, 83
pheasant and grouse shoots *see* animal protection
phronesis (practical judgement) 11
plants 106; charity workers and 77–8; genetic engineering and patenting *see separate entry*

INDEX

politics and ethics 105–6
postmodernism 14
primitivism 107
public campaigning 82–3
public health policy 23, 32, 39

racing society, Newmarket 9
Ragoné, H. 89, 90, 99
Rapp, R. 95
recycling 27
religion 109–10
responsibility as phenomenon of specific relations 78–9
Reynolds, A. F. P. 45
Rigby, K. 77
Ritte, W. 46, 48, 49, 51, 52, 55
Robbins, J. 10, 11
Roberts, E. F. S. 90
Roberts, M. 45, 51, 57
Romans 108
Rousseau, J.-J. 35

Sahlins, M. 7, 52, 56, 58
Salmón, E. 51, 59
Save the Whale 9–10
Say, Calvin 50, 58–9
Schlais, K. G. 44, 45, 51, 56, 58
Schneider, D. M. 5, 6, 7
Schrire, M. 58
scientists *see* genetic engineering and patenting
Scotland: animal protection *see separate entry*; surrogacy and maternal bond *see separate entry*
Sears, W. and M. 21–2, 37, 38
self-reflexivity 107
sexual orientation 74
Shiva, V. 44
Shostak, M. 30
Sierra, Santiago 106
Small, M. 30
Smith, J. 50
Smith, M. 83–4
snaring *see* animal protection
social construction 5–6
socio-economic status 39; *see also* class
Song, H. 69, 72–3, 77, 82
sovereignty 60
Stanworth, M. 90

Stoett, P. J. 9
Stone, D. G. 45, 60
Storch, Bryna 'Oliko 50, 51, 60
storytelling 109–10, 111
Strathern, M. 3, 6, 13, 59, 70, 90, 100, 111
Suizzo, M.-A. 33–4, 91
surrogacy and maternal bond 14, 95–8, 100–1, 110; altruism 98–9; contracts 97; counselling 98; femininity 87, 90, 95, 99, 100; identity 91, 100, 101; kinship 87, 89–90, 91, 97, 100, 101; natural feeling 98–100; nature of motherhood 88–91; 'nine-month head-start' 86–8, 91, 94, 101; vital difference 91–5

Tanji, M. 51
taro (Colocasia esculenta) and Hawaii *see* genetic engineering and patenting
Teman, E. 89, 90
Thomas, N. 109
Thompson, C. 6, 7, 13, 89–90
Thurer, S. 21
totemism 8–9
traditional knowledge 48, 56
Trujillo, E. E. 46, 47, 49
Tsing, A. L. 6
Tsuji, Clift 50, 58–9
TT (a minor) 97
Turner, J. N. 51

United Kingdom: animal protection *see separate entry*; childbirth 27; green movement 8; 'natural' breastfeeding: case studies in London and Paris *see* breastfeeding; Newmarket racing society 9; surrogacy and maternal bond *see separate entry*
United Nations Declaration on the Rights of Indigenous Peoples 45
United States 21, 24, 27, 28, 33, 35; Bayh-Dole Act (1980) 57; infertility clinics 89–90; surrogacy 89–90, 99; taro (Colocasia esculenta) and Hawaii *see* genetic engineering and patenting
urbanisation 27

INDEX

vaccination 27
Valenzuela, Hector 57–8

Wall, G. 91
Warner, J. 33, 34
Warnock, M. 96
Wells, J. 28, 29
wet-nursing 35, 89, 90
whaling 9–10
Whitt, A. L. 45
Williams, R. 7, 99

World Health Organization (WHO) 23, 32
Wyndham, F. 51

Yanagisako, S. 6, 7
Yearley, S. 7
Yuen, L. 46

Zipper, J. 90
Żmijewski, Artur 106
zoo animals 74